DAILY WORD for Women

365 Days of Love, Inspiration, and Guidance

Written and edited by Colleen Zuck,
Janie Wright, and Elaine Meyer

BERKLEY BOOKS, NEW YORK

A Berkley Book
Published by The Berkley Publishing Group
A division of Penguin Putnam Inc.
375 Hudson Street
New York, New York 10014

PRINTING HISTORY
Rodale Press hardcover edition published in 1999
Berkley trade paperback edition / April 2000

ISBN: 0-425-17227-9

Visit our website at
www.penguinputnam.com

PRINTED IN THE UNITED STATES OF AMERICA

14   13   12   11   10   9

An Invitation

Daily Word is the magazine of Silent Unity, a worldwide prayer ministry now in its second century of service. Silent Unity believes that:

◆ *all people are sacred*
◆ *God is present in all situations*
◆ *everyone is worthy of love, peace, health, and prosperity*

Silent Unity prays with all who ask for prayer. Every prayer request is held in absolute confidence, and there is never a charge. You are invited to contact Silent Unity 24 hours a day, any day of the year.

Write: Silent Unity, 1901 NW Blue Parkway
Unity Village, MO 64065-0001
Or call: (816) 969-2000   Fax: (816) 251-3554
Online: http://www.silentunity.org

There's More!

If you enjoy these inspirational messages, you may wish to subscribe to *Daily Word* magazine and receive a fresh, contemporary, uplifting message for each day of the month. With its inclusive, universal language, this pocket-size magazine is a friend to millions of people around the world.

For a free sample copy or for subscription information regarding *Daily Word* in English (regular and large-type editions) or in Spanish, please write:

Silent Unity, 1901 NW Blue Parkway
Unity Village, MO 64065-0001
Or call: (800) 669-0282   Fax: (816) 251-3554
Online: http://www.dailyword.org

LIST OF ARTICLES

Giving Unconditional, Uncritical Love 31
by Betty White

Love Heals. 62
by Jessie O'Neill

The Healing Gift of Laughter 93
by Phyllis Diller

The Power of Words 125
by Mary-Alice Jafolla

A Second Chance. 156
by Sister Mary Rose Christy

The Brighter Outcome. 187
by Jayne Meadows

God's Gift of Life! 220
by Maya Brandenberger

The Gift of God's Love 251
by Lynne Brown

Creating a New Life of Love. 282
by Dee Wallace Stone

A Glimpse of the Eternal. 315
by Joan Lauren

Reaching Out to Children. 346
by Marian Wright Edelman

The Power of Love. 382
by Cheryl Landon

INTRODUCTION—
NOURISHING YOUR SOUL

As surprising as it may seem, many of us may be undernourished—probably not physically, for we nourish our bodies daily with food. We plan meals, shop for food, and cook what we hope are well-balanced, healthful meals for ourselves and our families. Collecting and trading recipes, talking about food, and eating meals are a part of our daily rituals.

Certainly, we try never to neglect the nourishment of our minds. We understand that we are on a lifelong quest in which every day we learn something through reading, listening, observing, and experiencing life. In our homes and communities, through our families and careers, we use what we have learned in myriad roles: as spouses, parents, friends, teachers, advisors, or caregivers.

Where we might be undernourished is in our souls. If any of us are in doubt about this, let's ask ourselves how many times we have prayed, meditated, or taken a minute or two to stop whatever we are doing, just be still, and then become aware of the presence of God within. How much of our reading and conversation is about what is holy and sacred about us and about others?

Whether we are spiritually starved or just a little bit hungry, we will find a banquet to nourish our souls every day as we read this book. There are 365 soul-enriching messages, plus some true-life experiences of women like us that will bring us greater insight into how our souls can be nourished daily, no matter what we are going through—crisis, loss, achievement, or discovery.

Each day, we will read a quote from a woman who shines the light of understanding on what is both practical and inspirational. By reading the daily message that follows the quote, we open our minds and hearts to the sacredness of our souls. Here we come face-to-face, so to speak, with both our humanity and our sacredness so that we know we are whole and holy. The messages end with a simple, but powerful, statement—an affirmation—which we may choose to use throughout the day whenever we need a spiritual boost.

After a six-day series of messages, we are offered a "God message" written as an encouragement for us to recognize how God would sound, speaking directly to us. We will discover that we are much stronger and wiser than we ever before realized, because what we are reading is written as pure, unconditional love. We understand that when God talks to us, we hear love talking to us, for God is love.

How to Use This Book

You may want to start with message one and read a message a day, or you can read several messages each day. You may choose to search through the titles of daily messages for one that especially appeals to you, like "Turning Point," "Healing Life," "Quiet of Prayer," or "Laughter."

Any time during the day is a good time to nurture the soul. Yet, like others, you may find that how you start the day sets the tone for the whole day, and morning is the time for a fresh start. Then you can put what you have read to practice throughout the day. You may choose to read in the evening, sleep on it, and then apply what you have read to your life the next day.

Listen as you read the "God messages" of love. They are there to acclimate you to how God would sound talking to you, encouraging you. Love will always bring out the best in you, reminding you that even if you feel low, there is still great strength and wisdom just waiting to be expressed by you. Then listen in the quiet of your own being for Love to speak to you, building your courage in times of crisis and celebrating with you in your times of achievement.

Every seventh day you will be offered a Bible scripture, and perhaps you will choose to read a few lines before or after that verse. Or maybe you will decide to read the whole chapter. The version of the Bible used here is the New Revised Standard Version, but if you prefer, you may read another version.

Read the stories of other women, like the heartwarming story of how actor Michael Landon's daughter Cheryl discovered the power of love through her relationship with her father. And you will probably hear her laughter as actress/comedienne Phyllis Diller explains the healing power in laughter.

Once you have read the whole book, you may want to set it aside for a while or you may want to start rereading it. Like those of us who wrote and edited this book, you, too, will gain new insight and inspiration from each page each time you read it. Then continue to nourish your soul every day by knowing that you have all you need to live a fulfilling, healthy, peaceful, and enriched life.

—The Editors

Day 1

—◆—

*The world is round and the place which may seem
like the end may also be the beginning.*
—*Ivy Baker Priest*

**TURNING
POINT**
This day is a turning point in my life. My joy, my peace of mind, and my reality are no longer controlled by anyone or anything outside of me. This is the day I begin living my life from the inside out. And I am transformed!

The thoughts I think and the plans I make are ones that are encouraged and empowered by the spirit of God within me. I am helping to create my own life rather than letting the quality and richness of my life be decided by what is happening to me and around me.

Yes, this is how it feels to live from the faith and joy of my soul! Moment by moment, I am being transformed from the inside out. As I live from the peace of God within me, I feel the transformation that is happening within me. I see it on my face and I hear it in my voice.

**I live my life from the inside out—from the spirit
of God within me.**

Day 2

—◆—

God is in us as the very life and substance that we use. . . . God is life; we make that life into living.—*Myrtle Fillmore*

HEALING LIFE

God's spirit is within me; I know this is true. The spirit of God is eternal, continually enlivening me and restoring me. Cell by cell, breath by breath, heartbeat by heartbeat, I am being renewed.

There is a deep satisfaction that comes from being an active participant in healthful living. Out of a reverence for life, I give myself the consideration, care, and understanding that I would give any other creation of God.

I give thanks for health of mind and body: "Thank You, God, for a heart that was created to beat in perfect rhythm, for lungs designed to breathe in the breath of life, for a body that was fashioned to be both strong and flexible. With every breath I take, with every beat of my heart, I am refreshed and renewed. Thank You, God, for life!"

The healing life of God restores and enlivens me now!

Day 3

—◆—

Hope is the thing with feathers
That perches in the soul.
—Emily Dickinson

HOPE

I am learning that it is one thing to anticipate the best possible outcome and quite another to know exactly what that outcome should be. Yet what I know with even greater conviction is that I can always dare to hope. I can when my hopes and dreams are from the understanding that God is the one presence and power in all the universe. I accept that God loves and cares for me.

I recognize why the accumulation of material things can never truly satisfy the hunger within me. What is becoming clear is that I am hungering to know God, to feel God's presence, to experience unconditional love.

So whenever I seem to be reaching out in desperation to someone or something, I know to turn to God within me. God is my hope and the satisfaction that I hunger for, the loving presence that is always waiting within me.

God is my hope and my soul satisfaction.

Day 4

—◆—

Prayer is made up of words filled with invisible power.
This is the greatest life-giving energy on Earth.
—Sue Sikking

HERE I AM

I asked, "God, please never leave me on my own." And the answer I received was a reassurance that came to me quicker than a heartbeat: "You and I can never be separated, for My spirit is the very life within you. I am with you always—for all eternity."

I continued to be quiet and listen—a way of praying without words, of lingering in a sacred atmosphere. I was aware of God with my whole being and filled with an undeniable feeling that I was sacred.

Then I said, "God, here are my hands. Let them give the gentle, sure touch that conveys love and caring in all that I do. God, here is my voice. Let me speak words that are kind and compassionate. God, here I am, ready to share the wonder of Your presence with everyone."

From the sacred atmosphere of my soul,
I awaken to the presence of God.

Day 5

—◆—

When one door of happiness closes, another opens;
but often we look so long at the closed door that we
do not see the one which has opened for us.
—Helen Keller

LETTING GO

How easy it is for me to stop thinking about something I am concerned about may depend on how serious I think the challenge is. Yet does worry ever really help? Never!

So I let go of worry and give my time and energy to what does help: I affirm my faith in God to guide and support me. The answers to the questions in my heart are found in the wisdom of God. I let go, knowing that God is ready to work through me and others to bring about what is best for all.

I believe prayer helps. I welcome the strength and assurance that I feel in being in communion with God. And I trust that my prayers reach out in a powerful and positive way to all those who are involved in the situation.

I let go and let God guide me.

Day 6

—◆—

Grace is God's gift of love and mercy,
given freely to us whether or not
we deserve it.—Hypatia Hasbrouck

GRACE
Grace is the love of God in action. And it is grace that inspires me to be loving. What delight I feel in knowing that no matter what has happened in the past, I can begin right now to let God love through me. With a willingness to be open to grace moving through me, I am encouraged to love and be loved.

Grace brings me such peace of mind. When I stop to realize that no blessing will ever be withheld from me, I catch a glimpse of the magnitude of God's love. God is always giving me a way to live more fully and to love more completely.

In silence, there is a sacred place where love and peace, in their purest forms, await me. Through the grace of God, I have access to these qualities, and God shows me how to weave them into the very fabric of my daily life.

By the grace of God, I am "love" reaching out to others.

Day 7

—◆—

Beloved,

You are precious to Me. You always have been and always will be. I love you and I will always love you.

My creation of you did not stop when you were born into this world. You were not finished then, nor are you finished now. You have far to go. But if you grow weary, remember that I am with you and I will carry you. You have so much to discover! May you find joy in each thought that connects you consciously with My life within you. May you discover wisdom with each feeling that brings you a clearer understanding of your own spiritual identity.

Each time you face a challenge with faith, you help to light up the world with sacred awareness. And what a light of hope you are! So, My beloved, let the light of My spirit within you shine as you continue to learn and grow, to hope and trust. Yes, I am with you—always.

"I trust in the steadfast love of God forever and ever."—Psalm 52:8

Day 8

— ◆ —

Do not follow where the path may lead.
Go instead where there is no path and
leave a trail.—Muriel Strode

M Y STORY

I may be confused sometimes about what my life is all about. If I were writing my life story, what would the plot be? Would life be an adventure, a mystery, a myth? What wisdom would I want to pass on to others?

The one constant in life is said to be change, which keeps life interesting. Yet I know that even more constant in my life is the presence of God. One day I may be going through a challenge, another day I have a success. Some days I feel on top of the world, and some days I seem to be at the bottom, needing the love and comfort that only the supreme Presence can give me.

My life is the unfolding story of a creation of God. Oh, what a blessing it is to be alive, to have God accompany me through life! What a story God is telling through me!

I am the unfolding story of one of God's creations!

Day 9

—◆—

If you want to accomplish goals in your life,
you have to begin with spirit.
—Oprah Winfrey

SACRED PARTNERSHIP I recognize that the disappointment I feel in not doing my best or being my best is an encouragement to do better. How can I do better? I can by knowing that I am not going it alone. I am living my life in partnership with God. Nothing is too insignificant to talk to God about; nothing is too monumental for God and I to handle together.

I sense an eagerness building within me. I know intuitively that creative, exceptional ideas are waiting for me to act upon them. My best intentions are ready to be launched into productive actions.

What seemed only yesterday to be a hopeless situation is now an opportunity for me to let God express wisdom and creativity through me to bring about marvelous results.

God is expressing wisdom and creativity
through me now!

Day 10

—◆—

*Faith works on and on
after all reason is exhausted.*
—Cora Dedrick Fillmore

NEW BEGINNINGS Whenever I come to a turning point in my life—a new beginning for me— I meet it with faith. There is a divine plan at work in my life, and I know that every new beginning will contain something of meaning and value for me.

I am making progress in my growing awareness of my own spirituality. With freedom of spirit, I accept the changes that appear as beginnings for me. I am ready for newness in life because God is constantly preparing me for life.

Releasing the past and focusing on the present moment, I embrace the wonder of today and remain open to the newness that is being offered me. Today and every day is a day of new beginnings and newfound wonders.

**I am ready for a new beginning and ready
to embrace the wonder of today.**

Day 11

—◆—

God stirs up our comfortable nests, and pushes us over the edge of them, and we are forced to use our wings. . . . Read your trials in this light, and see if your wings are being developed.—*Hannah Whitall Smith*

COMFORT

God, You comfort me when I need love and understanding, and I want to be a messenger of peace and support to my friends and loved ones during their times of need.

God, Your love fills my heart and mind. I want the words of comfort I give to others to be Your message of love to the world. Just as You have done for me, I listen with patience to those whom I am comforting. Thank You for helping me share Your love with them.

One of the greatest comforts I can give to my loved ones is to listen and remind them that true peace of mind can only come from Your presence within. Through self-discovery, they, too, will recognize that You and You alone are the comfort that reaches down into their souls.

God gives me the comfort that reaches into my soul.

Day 12

◆

*All serious daring
starts from within.
—Eudora Welty*

ONE STEP   As a child, I learned to walk only after I had taken that first step. Then I learned to run. My first steps may have been unsteady, but with them I was on my way to discovering a whole new world filled with unlimited possibilities.

Each day is a new journey, and I take the first step by trusting God to show me the way. Yes, there may be shortcuts, and I discover these with joy and expectation. And I am also prepared to take side trips along the way, for it is in the unexpected that I often find the most inspiration.

Right now, as I begin the new journey that this day holds for me, I can put aside all doubt and know that wherever I am going, God is with me—each and every step of the way.

Each road to success begins with the first step.

Day 13

—◆—

Prayer is when you talk to God;
meditation is when you listen to God.
—Diana Robinson

SACRED PRAYER   At any time, in any situation, prayer is an effective and powerful way for me to focus on God, the one true source of all there is. Prayer is my eternal link to all that is pure, all that is timeless, all that is true—my stepping-stone over troubled waters and onto a foundation of immense spiritual support.

During my sacred times of prayer, I ask for guidance. In the quietness of my soul, I receive the comfort and support I seek. God knows my innermost thoughts and dreams even before I realize what they are. Long before I ask, God has ready for me the guidance to the fulfillment of a divine plan.

One with God, I am one with my friends, my family—with all creation. I am an important part of the complete whole that is God. In sacred prayer, I quiet my own thoughts and listen.

In my sacred times of prayer,
I listen to God.

Day 14

—◆—

Beloved,

Throughout all eternity, I am with you. Whenever you need Me, I am there, ready to give you the love, the comfort, and the strength you need.

As you pray, then listen, then step out in faith, you are living from a glorious realization of your oneness with Me and with all of My beloved creations. Never forget this connection, for with it you can reach seemingly miraculous heights of achievement.

Every day is a new chapter in the story of your life. And every day you are becoming more aware of your partnership with Me. Enjoy this sacred time and remember this truth: As you let My love shine brightly within you, you are a beacon of love and light to the world.

"I am with you always."
—Matthew 28:20

Day 15

—◆—

The prayers we make for others are twofold in their action:
They reach and bless and help the one for whom we pray;
they act in us . . . to give us peace.—Martha Smock

PRAY FOR OTHERS The solution to a problem may seem so much easier when I am not directly involved in the challenging situation. And I probably have some good ideas about how to resolve it—if only someone would listen!

No matter how good my intentions or my advice may be, there is still a better way: I turn the situation and the person over to God in prayer and cooperate with a divine solution. I send my dear one a message of love and faith:

"I love you, I bless you, and I behold you enfolded in God's loving light. I trust God to lead you on your own unique journey.

"I will always do what I can for you, but I know that God and you will do so much better. In all you do, I know you are being blessed."

I am praying with and for my loved ones today.

Day 16

—◆—

Instead of thinking about where you are,
think about where you want to be.
—Diana Rankin

I Am More

Sometimes, in an almost mystical experience, I find that in doing less and saying less, I become more. I am more because I am rising above preconceived ideas about how things must be or how I should act. I am in the flow of a powerful, sacred stream of consciousness when I allow the peace, love, and understanding of God within me to be the source of all that I am and all that I do.

I understand that my real role in life is that of a spiritual being of light and love. And I am being true to myself when I am being true to the spiritual being that I am. I am doing my best and being my best when I rely on God, and I receive confirmation as I hear God whispering to me, "You are My beloved child."

Living my life as a spiritual being, I am
doing my best and being my best!

Day 17

—◆—

Him that I love, I wish to be free—
even from me.
—Anne Morrow Lindbergh

FREE

Whether I am making decisions about everyday responsibilities or important goals, I have freedom of choice. And it is incredibly important for me to remember that making choices is a freedom, not a burden. God is assisting me in every choice I make—from household decisions to establishing priorities in my career. But my most important choice is to follow God's guidance.

Regardless of what is happening to me at any one time in my life, I can make the choice to follow God by acting in ways that reflect the light and love of God within me. Because I have made this choice, I will experience freedom from unproductive habits and limitations.

My prayer is a declaration of choice: "God, I give thanks for Your loving presence. It is my choice to follow You and be a worthy expression of Your spirit."

God, I give thanks for Your loving presence in my life.

Day 18

———◆———

*I suppose the pleasure of country life lies really
in the eternally renewed evidences of
the determination to live.—Vita Sacksville-West*

FRESH

God's spirit is within me—now and always. Yet there may be times when the stress and anxieties of everyday living threaten to overwhelm me, times when I feel less than the whole and holy creation I am.

Maybe all I need is a little rest. Or it could be that I need to step back and look at my life from a perspective of wholeness and holiness. Then, whatever action I decide to take, the result will be the same: a fresh, new me who is ready and willing to get on with this adventure called life!

Through the spirit of God within me, I am renewed! My mind is open to God's guidance, and I am eager to get started now! I am renewed and strong and ready to receive all the blessings God has prepared for me.

**Through the spirit of God within me,
I am renewed!**

Day 19

*Trust in God
and do something.*
—Mary Lyon

**DIVINE
ORDER**

Two simple words—divine order—
yet how powerful they are when I
state them with conviction and belief!
Am I weary or in need of a healing?
By affirming the words *divine order*, I am taking my mind
off illness and limitation so that thoughts of healing can
rush in to aid me. I focus on the life of God as it surges
throughout my body, renewing and revitalizing me.

Do I seek greater freedom in my life or a better
way to live? Divine order! The spirit of God is always
with me, infusing my mind with the understanding I
need to accept my freedom or to make the necessary
improvements in my life.

No matter what I may need, I trust God and know
that divine order is always with me. When I put my
trust in God, I am amazed at the way everything falls
into place—all in divine order.

**Divine order is my affirmation of health, wisdom,
and prosperity.**

DAILY WORD FOR WOMEN

Day 20

—◆—

Ask God's blessing on your work,
but don't ask Him to do it for you!
—Dame Flora Robson

DIVINE GIFTS

At times it may seem as if I am rising up from the ashes of my own life because I have gone through an unhappy experience. Problems in relationships or on the job can take their toll both emotionally and physically. Yet I can rise up again and be the whole, free, and fulfilled person God created me to be.

When I am feeling weak, God within me is my strength. When I am going through a time of confusion, God within me is my wisdom. When I seem lost and alone, God within me lets me know that I can never be separated from divine life, love, and care.

Out of the ashes of the past, new life, new love, and new opportunities spring forth. And if I listen carefully and faithfully, I will hear that still small voice reminding me that these gifts are mine to have and to enjoy.

I receive the gifts of life, love, and opportunity from God.

Day 21

—◆—

Beloved,

Look at the people around you with spiritual awareness and see that, like you, they are truly expressions of My love reaching out to the world. Recognizing the sacredness of all life brings you a greater realization of your own sacredness and your capacity to be all that you dreamed you could be and even more!

Everything that is happening to you will lead you to the experiences that will help you to grow and give expression to your own unique gifts. Through it all, I am with you.

I am with you as you let go of the past, as you let go of worries and stress and any painful memories. I am with you as you take that first step into a new life with a heightened awareness of the greatness within you.

Beloved, take that next step. Now is the perfect time.

"Now is the acceptable time."
—2 Corinthians 6:2

DAILY WORD FOR WOMEN

Day 22

—◆—

Taking joy in living
is a woman's best cosmetic.
—Rosalind Russell

JOY For a blessed moment, I allow myself to put aside worries and become still. Quieting my mind and relaxing my body, I immerse myself in the presence of God. In God's presence, I am aware of inner joy, and I feel a surge of gladness within me. Joy is within me, rising up in jubilation over God's magnificent presence.

What a glorious feeling! Surely nothing can compare to the joy I feel when I am truly aware of God's presence. I radiate with joy because I know that joy is my heritage, that happiness and love and peace are what God created me to express.

It doesn't really matter what is going on around me, because God is within me. With God, I know that all things are possible if only I believe. And I do! I do believe in joy. I do believe in the miraculous truth of God's presence in my life.

God's joy sings in my heart!

Day 23

—◆—

You are unique, and if that is not fulfilled
then something has been lost.
—Martha Graham

SPIRIT OF LIFE

Everyone is unique, in appearance and mannerisms, yet we also have something in common—an alikeness that comes from being expressions of God. The same universal life force which lives and moves and has its being in me is the same life which lives in all. The responsibility of each individual is to give free expression to the divine presence.

So I affirm: I am a wonderfully unique and precious creation of God. Spirit is the life force within me, guiding my thoughts, words, and actions. And when I allow the spirit of God to flow uninhibited, it will radiate life and strength and wisdom throughout my being.

I am one with spirit and united with others in a bond of love. What is possible for one of us is possible for all of us, for we are imbued with the same innate power and presence.

I am one in spirit with God and one in spirit with every person in my life.

Day 24

—◆—

*I truly feel that there are as many ways of loving
as there are people in the world and as there are days
in the lives of those people.—Mary Calderone*

FORGIVE Every day, I renew a willingness
to forgive when I take the time to
respond to any situation in pure,
loving ways. And I open myself to the
wisdom of God when I forgive.

Each time I forgive, I move beyond the ups and
downs of my emotions into the peace-filled realm of
divine understanding. I become the pure, loving, and
gentle person I truly desire to be. I am willing to yield,
to be full of mercy. I think uplifting thoughts that lead
to a harvest of good.

In the atmosphere of forgiveness, I am refreshed and
my relationships are enhanced. When I forgive, I am
sowing seeds of peace, understanding, and acceptance
that promote loving, long-lasting relationships.

I express divine love each time I forgive.

Day 25

—◆—

I was always looking outside myself for strength . . .
but it comes from within. It is there all the time.
—Anna Freud

INNER PEACE   My prayers of peace are powerful messages of stress reduction that I send to my body every day:

"God, ever so gently I tell my body to relax so that Your peace within me will flow through me. Divine peace surges out from the core of my being and radiates throughout my digestive system, my heart, and my lungs.

"All concerns melt away in the warmth of Your peace, and the stress of the day now fades into a thing of the past. The muscles of my neck and back relax, and I know what it is like to be stress free. The same feeling of relaxation moves down my arms and legs, and inner peace fills my mind and body.

"Thank You, thank You, God, for peace that heals and restores me."

I give thanks for peace that heals and restores me.

DAILY WORD FOR WOMEN

Day 26

—◆—

You must do the thing
you think you cannot do.
—Eleanor Roosevelt

THRESHOLD   I stand on the threshold of a new day, a day in which I will discover or even rediscover my true spiritual nature.

I stand on the threshold of remembering—not just why I am here, but who I am in truth. I am on the brink of a momentous spiritual reawakening, and I am poised and ready to accept what lies before me.

What I am learning is, in fact, what I already know in my heart and soul—I am merely reattuning myself to the wisdom of Spirit.

My spoken prayers and my silent communion with God have brought me to this realization, and I eagerly await both spiritual and physical blessings. I am a child of God, and I claim my divine heritage—today!

I stand on the threshold of spiritual rediscovery.

Day 27

———— ◆ ————

*If you find it in your heart to care for somebody else,
you will have succeeded.*
—Maya Angelou

HARMONY When I take the time to remember that the spirit of God is present in every conversation I have with someone and that the spirit of God knows every thought I have about someone, how can any of my words or actions be anything but loving and considerate? How can my thoughts and plans be on anything but a high and positive level?

The answer to these questions is this: Because God is everywhere present, whatever I think about people, say to people, or do for people is always in the presence of God. So I bring harmonious words, thoughts, and acts to my interactions with others.

I live in harmony with the presence of God. I honor the holy presence within myself and within others by bringing harmony to every situation.

**I live in harmony because I live in
the presence of God.**

Day 28

—◆—

Beloved,

Do you know that you are loved? Never forget that My love is far beyond any love that you have ever before experienced.

Within you is the key that unlocks the door to the riches of My kingdom—your divine heritage of joy and peace, unity and harmony. And the key that unlocks these treasures is forged from your discovery of the spiritual power I have given you.

With faith in Me, you can experience your own spiritual awakening. Trust in Me. Have faith in My wisdom and power. Love Me and all that I have created. And remember—I, too, have faith in you.

"Blessed be the name of God . . .
He reveals deep and hidden things."
—Daniel 2:20, 22

Day 29

— ◆ —

Put your ear down close to your soul
and listen hard.
—Anne Sexton

NEW LOOK I may tend to view the world through opinions formed from my personal experiences and accumulated thoughts of a lifetime and then react accordingly. So how can I look at things from a positive perspective?

The answer is by keeping my thoughts on God, the source of all good. When I consider how God views the world, I naturally look at everything with appreciation for the Master's touch. I look at my world through eyes of love. As I do so, I rediscover the blessings I already have, such as the love of family and friends, the beauty of nature, the comfort of my home, and the richness of planet Earth.

As I give my life and my world a new look, I will find more and more reasons to celebrate and be thankful.

I look at the world around me and discover
new joy in living.

Day 30

*I move through my day-to-day life with a sense
of appreciation and gratitude that comes from knowing
how fortunate I truly am, and how unearned all that I am
thankful for really is.—Jean Shinoda Bolen*

PROSPERITY

As I consider the natural wonders of the world and the delicate balance of nature, it is easy for me to remember that the kingdom of God is all around me. Not at some future date and time, but right now, right where I am, I have the kingdom of God's abundant blessings!

That divine realm of blessings is within also—as comfort, love, understanding, and so much more. The kingdom of God cannot be contained, for it reaches out as love—a special gift from God that I can share with family and friends. I have life—healing life—and all the guidance and inspiration I will ever need.

Above all else, I have peace of mind. I know that God's loving presence is the mainstay of my existence. With joy in my heart, I accept abundant blessings.

It is God's good pleasure to give me the kingdom.

GIVING UNCONDITIONAL, UNCRITICAL LOVE
BY BETTY WHITE

When I was first introduced to Panda—a beautiful little shih tzu dog—she was being held in a cage, where she remained for the first six months of her life. She was impounded as evidence in an animal cruelty case, and I was not allowed to adopt her until the trial was over. I thought she would be so traumatized by her experience that she would have no sense of what it was like to be loved. I envisioned her as this frightened little puppy, cowering down to the two male dogs already in my home.

Was I ever wrong—on both counts. When I brought her home, Panda walked up to my dogs Timmy and Cricket as if to say, "All right, boys. Here's how it's going to be from now on: I'm running this show!" And believe me, she does!

Panda has never let her harsh beginning get in the way of her being a pure expression of unconditional love. And she is a constant reminder for me not to get discouraged. She helps me hang on to my faith, to that arrow pointing to the positive. She's a help not only for me, but for the people and animals around me.

Day 31

—◆—

Doing the best at this moment puts you
in the best place for the next moment.
—Oprah Winfrey

HOLY PRESENCE God, as I begin this day with thoughts of love and appreciation for You, I resolve to remain focused on Your truth. No matter what this day holds in store for me, Your love for me is constant, and Your care for me is all-pervading.

You are my constant companion, preparing the way for all my tomorrows to be positive and fruitful. I feel confident and my mind is free of any thoughts or memories that might control or limit me.

Whether I go out into the familiar world of my own neighborhood or into a totally unfamiliar environment, I am never outside Your loving care. God, knowing that Your holy presence is within me and surrounding me, I am ready for a glorious day.

Wherever I go and whatever I do, I am
always in the love and care of God.

Day 32

—◆—

A master can tell you what he expects of you.
A teacher, though, awakens your own expectations.
—Patricia Neal

**G O D
I S I N
C H A R G E**

At times I may have felt as if my life was out of my control, as if I did not know what to do next. Then, suddenly, I realized the way to regain composure was to know that God is in charge.

And with this realization, I did not feel as if I were giving up or giving in. On the contrary, when I surrender to God, I am affirming that God knows what is best, that God—the one power in the universe—is greater than any challenge I could ever face.

God created me to succeed and to be happy. And God is able to give me a road map that will take me around any obstacle. When I remember that God is in charge, I am assured that all is well.

God is in charge and all is well.

Day 33

——◆——

What's important is focusing on living and breathing . . .
and keeping our energy high so we can make the world
a more vital place for others.—Alexandra Stoddard

SELF-IMAGE

How often do I hear my voice on an audiotape or see a photograph of myself and think, "That does not sound or look like me!"

My own view of myself is often completely different from the way others perceive me. But I recognize that my true self is divine, for I am created in the image and likeness of God.

By remaining attuned to the power of God within me, I know that all I do is in the light and love of God. I can always maintain a confident self-image regardless of what is happening to me, because I am filled with the peace and assurance of Spirit.

My self-image is the best it can be when I remember that I am created in the image and likeness of God.

I have a great self-image because I know that I have been created in the image of God.

Day 34

—◆—

*Am I willing to give up what I have
in order to be what I am not yet?*
—Mary Caroline Richards

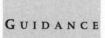

If I were walking down an unfamiliar path and came to a fork in the road, would I know which way to turn? Would I hesitate and spend fruitless hours pondering, "What if I went this way . . . or that way?"

No, I won't become stuck at a crossroad because I will always know my way in life when I turn to God and listen to divine guidance.

During my times of prayer, I give thanks for the guidance I have received and am always receiving. God knows my thoughts before I think them, my actions before I take them. Whether or not I am fully aware of it, God has always been giving me just the guidance I need.

I feel such confidence and security in knowing that wherever I go, God goes with me. I need never feel lost or alone, frightened or confused, because divine light and love shine before me, making my way clear.

God is continually guiding me.

Day 35

—◆—

Beloved,

When I look at you, I see beyond what you would see in the mirror. Viewing you as the loving parent that I am, I see you just as I created you to be—a perfect expression of unconditional love and unqualified beauty.

There is an abundance of joy and love within you. Let them be your guides to experiencing true peace and happiness.

As you listen to Me, let My words speak to your heart. Allow yourself to feel My love for you and know that you carry My spirit with you wherever you go.

"God saw everything that he had made, and indeed, it was very good."
—Genesis 1:31

Day 36

———◆———

One can never consent to creep
when one feels an impulse to soar.
—Helen Keller

REMEMBER New beginnings are times for setting goals, for letting go, and for looking to the future. But before I put the past behind me, I remember the important things I have learned:

I have learned through facing challenges that I am capable of dealing with whatever life presents to me. I have awakened to my own sacredness as a cherished child of God, loved unconditionally by God.

I have learned other things also—the importance of loving and letting others love me in return, the value of forgiveness in all of my relationships—all of which led to important breakthroughs in living.

Most important of all, I have learned that I can always start over, that each moment is a new beginning, ripe with possibilities.

**I remember the past and look forward
to a bright, new future.**

Day 37

— ◆ —

We can do no great things;
only small things with great love.
—Mother Teresa

MY SEARCH If I have been searching my heart and mind for an answer concerning the well-being of a spouse, a child, or a friend but still cannot make a decision, what do I do?

My search is not over until I have searched my soul, until I have pushed aside facts and figures, advice and recommendations, and simply asked, "God, what is the answer?"

Then I let Spirit bring the best resolution to my conscious awareness. The decision I am to make may come to my attention when I am in prayer or at rest, when I am in some activity or in conversation.

There is a surge of spiritual energy that identifies the decision so that I know, "Yes! This is it!" Even if doubts resurface, I will make the best decision because I am including God in my search.

All my worthwhile searching brings me back to God.

Day 38

—◆—

*Every new spiritual realization makes finer
and stronger and more beautiful the texture of the soul.*
—Cora Dedrick Fillmore

**POWER
OF GOD**
There is, perhaps, nothing that can uplift me more than prayer. Whether I literally get down on my knees, speak a prayer from Scripture, or silently linger in the presence of God, I feel relieved, as if a weight has been taken from me.

Prayer, for me, can be as simple as releasing concerns and worry and inviting God to fill my soul with love, peace, and understanding. There is nothing complicated about my giving over to the holy presence all that would come between me and an awareness of my Creator.

Prayer is surrendering any need to prove myself and knowing that I can prove the power of God.

**Through prayer, I experience the power
of God moving through me.**

Day 39

—◆—

The fragrance always stays in the hand
that gives the rose.
—Hada Bejar

BEING A FRIEND

Granted, I can never make a first impression with the same person more than once, but each day brings new opportunities to interact with people I have never met before or with whom I may never cross paths again. So I make it a point to be friendly and compassionate to everyone.

Because I am an expression of God, I use these opportunities to put my best self forward. Walking down a street, talking on a telephone, shopping in a store—wherever there are people to meet and interact with, that is where I greet people with a smile and treat them with respect.

I may not know where life will take me or my loved ones, but I can make a point of being the best person I can be. I am doing my part by being a friend in all of my interactions with others.

Thank You, God, for every opportunity
to be a friend.

Day 40

—◆—

When I stand before God at the end of my life, I would hope that I would not have a single bit of talent left, and could say, "I used everything you gave me."
—Erma Bombeck

GIFTS OF SPIRIT

God loves me and has given me unique gifts of talents and abilities. Through the love of God in me, the ways that I can benefit the world will open up to me.

Even if I am not sure what my gifts may be, I can be sure that I am using them. How? By the way I give—from my heart. Perhaps I have the sacred responsibility of caring for children or adults. My gifts may be the wisdom, patience, and strength to be caring.

Other gifts could be my ability to uplift someone who is feeling down or to bring new light to a complex problem. Whatever my gifts are, I know that they are vitally needed, vitally important to God's plan. Through love, I touch the heart of each individual I meet.

I have my own unique gifts to give to the world.

Day 41

———— ◆ ————

Wherever you are, you are in the presence
of God. . . . God is with you.
—Martha Smock

H O L D
O N !

There may be times when it is hard
to hold on to my faith—times when it
seems that there is no way out of a
situation or that my heartfelt prayers
are not being answered.

Then a gentle urging encourages me not to give up
and inspires me to hold on to my faith no matter what.
So I wait and listen and watch. Then I understand—
God was with me all along! I was never alone, never
without God's love and support as I made my way
through the darkest hour.

In fact, it was my faith that opened the door to God's
presence so that I was guided to a place of inner peace.
In every situation, my faith keeps me united with the
miracle-working power of God.

My faith unites me with the presence of God.

Day 42

—◆—

Beloved,

Your search for the answers to all your questions has not been in vain, for it brought you home to Me, to My presence within you. Now you know that divine wisdom is yours to express just by your acceptance of it. Divine power is yours to use as unlimited strength at any time, for it is moving through you at all times.

You are an expression of My love shining out into the world. Each time others catch a glimpse of your sacredness, they are encouraged to know that I am in you and also within them. What a blessing you are to Me and to the world.

It is My pleasure to be the love that reaches out from you and the wisdom that illuminates your mind. Be at peace in every moment of the day and night, for I will be there with you.

"When they call to me,
I will answer them."
—Psalm 1:15

Day 43
— ◆ —

Nobody has ever measured, not even poets,
how much the heart can hold.
—Zelda Fitzgerald

KINDNESS

I know that this is true for me:
When I am kind to others, I am the
first to be blessed.

This is because the kindness that I
give to anyone must first move through me, and it does
as a warm glow of love and acceptance emanating from
God's spirit within me. Kindness immediately refreshes
me with thoughts of what is highest and best.

That refreshing, relaxing feeling then moves
throughout my body, relieving me of any stored
tension, freeing my organs and muscles to function in
perfect ways.

I may not think that everyone deserves my kindest
thoughts, but I need to be blessed by them. For my
own well-being, I express kindness that heals and
refreshes me and all my relationships.

I am blessed by being kind to others.

Day 44

—◆—

It seems to me that those songs that have been any good,
I have nothing much to do with the writing of them.
The words have just crawled down my sleeve
and come out on the page.—*Joan Baez*

LOVING SPIRIT

Loving Spirit, I am placing my life in Your care and trusting Your wisdom to guide and inspire me. I trust You. Regardless of what others tell me to do or what appearances seem to suggest, I follow Your guidance. I know that Your wisdom is grounded in unconditional love for me and for all humankind.

Whether the decisions I have to make seem simple or complex, I listen to You. When I follow Your guidance, I am ensuring that what happens to me or to someone I care for is in the best interest of us all.

O loving Spirit, Your wisdom and understanding far surpass my greatest expectations, so I rely on You now and every day of my life. I am so very grateful for Your loving presence. I give thanks that You love me!

God's loving spirit guides and inspires me.

Day 45

—◆—

*Speak to God as if you were talking to your
very best and closest friend, because you are.*
—Mary-Alice Jafolla

**JOYFUL
AWAKENING**

Praying to God before I sleep
prepares me for a joyful awakening—
a feeling of excitement and expectation
about a new day.

In the first moments of that awakening, I have not
yet remembered what I was concerned about last night
or the day before. I am fresh, and joy moves through
me unimpeded.

I have awakened to life and to God in my life.
During the night while I slept, the spirit of God within
me was awake and active. As I slept, I gave Spirit access
to my consciousness and to even deeper levels of my
subconscious. God healed and refreshed me.

Joy rushes into my awakening moments and will
stay with me when I invite it to be a spirit of gladness
that permeates my whole day.

**Awakening to God is awakening to the joy
of God in my life.**

Day 46

—— ◆ ——

Love the moment, and the energy of
that moment will spread beyond all boundaries.
—Corita Kent

N o w ! Have I wanted to stop some negative habit or start a positive one, to reconcile with a loved one or begin a new friendship? What is holding me back? If I need more strength, then I call on the power of God within to accomplish whatever it is that will bless me and bless others. Yes! I have strength!

Do I lack the courage to do what I desire to do—to make a change or begin something new? Never, because as a child of God, there is no lack within me. When I begin to believe what is true about me, I feel courage welling up inside me. Yes! I have courage!

I have strength and courage. Now is the time to follow the inspiration of God, that gentle inner urging to live as the strong, wise, and loving person I am capable of being!

Yes, God, I am a strong, wise,
and loving person—now!

Day 47

—◆—

The condition of our outer world is always the perfect outpicturing of our inner world. If we do not like the picture we see, we can change it.—Margaret Ponders

NEW ME

This is such a special time in my life, for it is a time of reflection, a time for reflecting on my life's journey. I determine what has worked and what has not, what is helping me the most and what is no longer useful.

As I sort through the cubbyholes of my life, I sweep out the cobwebs and release what is no longer necessary—all in preparation for the new me that is beginning to emerge. In prayer, I affirm what I know is true—life, sweet blessed life—and release the "old" me.

"God, I welcome Your cleansing, renewing presence in my life. As Your spirit sweeps over my soul, I experience a feeling of newness and restoration. You guide each step I take as I grow and unfold in spiritual awareness."

I sweep out the cobwebs of my life and prepare for the new me that is emerging.

Day 48

— ◆ —

*What was the duty of the teacher
if not to inspire?*
—Bharati Mukherjee

ENRICHED LIFE There is a Native American saying that if you give a person a fish, you feed that person one meal; but if you teach a person how to fish, you feed him or her for a lifetime.

And it is true that understanding does enrich my life. Some of the greatest transforming experiences come out of the depths of challenges. Although the challenges I have experienced are not necessarily what I thought I needed to experience, I am wiser and my life is richer for having come through them.

This is because what truly enriches my life is what I give back to life through being aware of my own spirituality and the spirituality of all who live in God's abundant world.

God is the source of all that enriches me.

Day 49

—◆—

Beloved,

Every moment of every day is a glorious new beginning for you! And as you begin to appreciate even more the wonderful creation that you are, you will begin to see that your life is being enriched in ways beyond your wildest imaginings.

Each kind thought you think, each loving act you perform brings about a joyful new awakening. In your own mind and heart, there is an awakening as you open yourself to the love that resides within you. And there is an awakening in the minds and hearts of the people around you who are affected by what you say and do.

This is just the beginning—the beginning of a grand and glorious adventure in which you will discover just how wonderful you are!

"Wonderful are your works."
—Psalm 139:14

Day 50

—◆—

The only courage that matters is the kind
that gets you from one moment to the next.
—Mignon McLaughlin

QUIET TALKS WITH GOD

In the quietness of my soul, I can turn to God for the strength and reassurance I need. As I listen, God speaks to me in a language my mind and heart can hear.

God walks with me, and I draw upon divine strength. The path I follow is one that God has created, so I do not fear what lies ahead. God is with me and leads me to a place of quiet solitude where I find the comfort I seek.

From the moment I first entered this physical realm, I was a part of God and I always will be. There are no limits to what God is and can do. Because I am God's beloved child, my heritage is a world of God's creation.

Through my quiet talks with God, I am comforted. In the quietness of my soul, I gain peace of mind and strength of spirit.

In the quietness of my soul, God speaks
to me of love and comfort.

Day 51

—◆—

*I give my life to learning
how to live.*
—Sandra Hochman

MIRACLE OF LIFE There are times when it is easy to maintain a powerful faith. Other times I pray that God will perform a miracle or give me a sign to let me know that I am on the right track.

Well, when I think about it, I don't need to look far, for I am a miracle! God created me in the divine image, with a mind and body that are capable of performing amazing feats. I am strong because the life of God lives within me. It renews and energizes me so that I am ready for optimal living. That is miraculous!

I am ready for a miracle, because miracles are happening all around me! Every bit of life is a testament to God's loving presence. And every bit of life is truly a miracle, a sign from God that tells me I am, indeed, on the right track.

I am ready for a miracle!

Day 52

— ◆ —

Today the real test of power is not capacity
to make war but capacity to prevent it.
—*Anne O'Hare McCormick*

WORLD VISION

"Let there be peace on Earth, and let it begin with me." These words from a popular hymn remind me of my own responsibility in creating and maintaining peace—in my relationships, in my home, and in my workplace. The peace that begins with me moves out into the world.

So I do what I can to promote peace: I am loving and kind, and I live by the Golden Rule. But above all, I recognize the need to maintain a vision of peace on Earth, a vision of the world as God created it to be.

In my mind's eye, I see a world that is filled with love, a world where goodwill exists among all the nations. People are working together and helping one another without a thought for personal gain. Yes, God is everywhere, and I know that Earth is truly the home God lovingly prepared for us all.

I envision the world as God created it to be—
filled with peace and love.

Day 53

—◆—

*You can choose to be on the side of God
and so find an inner peace and tranquility that nothing
can disturb.—Martha Smock*

BLESSED ASSURANCE What attribute is such an inherent part of me that no person or event can take it away? What is so sacred to my soul that I alone can make the decision to recognize it and use it?

Inner peace—the assurance of God's presence in me and in my world—is mine and is active in my soul every moment of the day and night. With God, I can always find that peaceful point of calm in the midst of a crisis or that level of divine understanding I need in a time of great achievement.

Inner peace cannot be given to me by the events I participate in or by the people I love. Peace is the blessed assurance of God's unfailing presence in me and in my life. And always, deep within my soul, peace is waiting to be united with my thoughts and lived in my life.

**Inner peace comes forth to be united
with my thoughts and lived in my life.**

Day 54

—◆—

All things are to be examined and called
into question. There are no limits set on thought.
—Edith Hamilton

THOUGHTS OF HEALING Whenever I need a healing—physically, mentally, or emotionally—I know that a positive attitude can be just the right boost to get me on my way to feeling better. To bring my awareness to this positive point of view, I keep my thoughts focused on the life of God that is constantly at work in me as healing energy.

Every cell of my body is alive with divine energy. My body tingles with the activity of the divine life that is moving throughout me. Even before I am aware that a healing might be in order, I know that God-life within is already actively at work.

Because I know that healing is taking place, my mind is filled with thoughts of health and wholeness, and I picture myself strong and vitally alive.

God-life moves through me as healing energy.

Day 55

—◆—

*I prefer liberty to chains
of diamonds.*
—Lady Mary Wortley Montagu

DAY OF INDEPENDENCE

O sacred Spirit, fill me with Your loving presence and show me the way to true freedom and lasting peace.

Teach me how to let go of the past by releasing the worries, the fears, the doubts, and the pain that can only keep me from living fully now.

I feel Your love supporting me as I begin and continue to overcome any habit that might weigh me down or slow my spiritual progress. This is my own personal independence day because I realize that I no longer need to rely on negative habits or ways I may have relied on in the past. You give me the courage to make transforming changes in myself.

Thank You, God, for guiding me, inspiring me, comforting me, and filling me with Your peace. Aware of Your holy spirit, I gladly give up the old ways for a new and better way.

God's holy spirit sets me free!

Day 56

—◆—

Beloved,

You have given Me your complete trust, and I have shown you the miracle that you are. Now, as you prepare to take this understanding with you out into the world, hold on to your vision of what the world can be, hold on to what you know is true.

Remain steadfast in your faith so that you may receive My blessed assurance—the assurance of my presence and the assurance that all is well.

Keep a vision of yourself being uplifted to a higher place than you ever thought you could possibly reach. And in the process of uplifting yourself, you will help uplift those around you.

You are such an integral part of the world in which you live! Through your every thought, word, and action, you are making a difference and declaring that each day is a celebration for every child of God!

"I press on toward the goal for the prize
of the heavenly call of God."
—Philippians 3:14

Day 57

—◆—

Prayer does not use any artificial energy, it
doesn't burn up any fossil fuel, it doesn't pollute.
—*Margaret Mead*

SANCTUARY OF THE SOUL

In the course of a day, I will probably hear the voices of many people—some full of cheer and joy, perhaps some with traces of negativity. But the one true voice I turn to for guidance and wisdom is the voice of Spirit.

In prayer, I enter into the sanctuary of my soul and rest in the presence of infinite Spirit. All the emotions that were my reactions to life are left at the gate of my inner sanctuary. I bring nothing with me but quietness.

Even though I leave everyone else behind when I enter the sanctuary of my soul, I am never alone. Spirit is with me. As I become still and listen, the spirit of God speaks to me. My questions are answered and my mind is at ease. I am strengthened and at peace.

As I listen in the sanctuary of my soul,
Spirit speaks to me.

Day 58

———◆———

*Rest is only a space of time from our ceaseless activities
and growth so that God can give us . . . a new dream,
new ideas, new accomplishments, new mountains
to want to climb.—Stella Terrill Mann*

FOUNDATION The biggest, most magnificent
building is only as strong as the
foundation on which it is built. To
support story after story, the
foundation must be strong.

And if I pattern my life by using my faith as the
foundation on which to build, then everything in my
life will be created in harmony with God.

Each day is built upon the strength of what I
accomplished and learned the day before. Even though
I am constantly building as I learn and grow from all of
my experiences, my unshakable foundation of faith in
God will always remain steadfast and supportive. All
that I build upon my foundation of faith will be in
harmony with a divine plan.

My life is in harmony with the nature of God.

DAILY WORD FOR WOMEN

Day 59

—◆—

Those who are lifting the world upward and onward
are those who encourage more than criticize.
—Elizabeth Harrison

MY HEART SINGS
The best thing I can do for my loved ones is to pray for them, and the best prayers I can say are prayers that are filled with heartfelt joy and unconditional love.

My heart sings with joy, and I celebrate! I celebrate because I know that every person in my life—family, friend, co-worker, or acquaintance—is a beloved child of God who is infused with the spirit of God. And nothing can come between any person and his or her blessings from God.

God's love is unconditional, and this is the love I give to others when I pray for them. I do not judge or condemn, but rather give understanding and forgiveness. In prayer, I give thanks for my family and friends and for everyone on Earth. With a joy-filled heart, I bless them in my prayers.

My prayers for others are prayers of love and joy.

Day 60
——◆——

We have to have little milestones in our days when we stop and really live in the moment and acknowledge that life is made up of these ordinary moments.
—Naomi Judd

IN GOD'S HAND I find such comfort when I envision myself being taken by the hand and led on safe pathways by God. Aware of the presence of God, I am alert to potential problems and follow through with the appropriate action or inaction. My first step in whatever I plan is to take God's hand in prayer:

"God, I am sensitive to Your touch, so I feel guided at every crossroad and in every time of decision. You give me a gentle nudge in the right direction and surround me with Your presence.

"There is no decision that I must make alone, for You are always with me. On the darkest night, You light my way. On the stormiest day, You provide me with shelter. Thank You, thank You, God."

Before I make any plan, I turn to God in prayer.

LOVE HEALS
BY JESSIE O'NEILL

I n helping myself with my recovery from alcoholism, I decided to do what I could to heal my relationship with my father. I began by trying not to let his drunken conversations over the phone upset me. Usually they left me angry and depressed for days, sometimes weeks.

Finally, in an effort to begin the process of forgiveness, I began to end each phone conversation with, "I love you, Daddy."

When I first started doing this, he would hang up on me. Then, after maybe a year, he started grunting, "Hmm," and then would slam down the phone. After another year, he started saying, "Me, too," and would then gently hang up. A few years into our healing, he would say, "I love you too, honey."

Later, after my father died, I learned that he had often told his friends, "My daughter and I never hang up the phone without saying 'I love you' to each other." And Daddy was right.

Day 61

◆

Life is love, enjoy it. Life is mystery, know it.
Life is a promise, fulfill it.
—Mother Teresa

HEALING LIFE

Being healthy means being well—mentally as well as physically. Thinking creative, positive thoughts lays the groundwork necessary for maintaining health and for reclaiming health. I keep my body strong and healthy with a balance of proper nutrition, regular exercise, and plenty of rest.

But there is something that I can do that is even more vital to my health and total well-being: I pray. Prayer is the key that opens the door to mind and body renewal. As I enter into prayer—the quiet, peaceful realm where all things are possible—I feel tension leave my muscles and stressful thought lift from my mind. Peace and calm immediately fill the void left behind, and I feel renewed. God is my health and strength of both mind and body. I am refreshed and restored.

The healing life of God renews my mind and body.

Day 62

—◆—

*No matter what you choose, you always have
to take a leap of faith.*
—Christiane Northrup

**LEAP
OF FAITH**

God, I know that whenever I try to hold onto love as if I am going to lose it, I am, in effect, thwarting the expression of my own love.

I realize that when I try my hardest to control a situation, that is when I feel as if I am losing control.

When I experience an inner urging to move forward in my life or career but don't even take the first step, I know that I am letting doubt be an anchor.

God, I know that when I let go of concern or fear, You are there to support me in being loving, in making decisions, and in taking leaps of faith. So I let go of what has been or what might have been and let You show me something even better. How alive I feel letting You be God in my life!

**God, I let You be God in my life,
and I feel alive and fulfilled!**

Day 63

—◆—

Beloved,

Listen—do you hear a message being whispered in your soul, a gentle urging for you to discover more about yourself and the divine power that lies within you?

You share a divine heritage with all people on Earth. This divine inheritance is the answer to every need: My presence and My power are with you in every moment. As you feel a gentle breeze that caresses your face, think of Me. As you gaze upon the beauty and majesty of nature all around you, see My wonder. Listen to the laughter and joy of your family and friends, and know that I am with you.

I am your creator and your sustainer, and you will never have to make any journey alone. That urging to discover the power within you was your desire to discover more of Me.

"Call, and I will answer."
—Job 13:22

Day 64

—◆—

Lifting the veil of fear allows us to see the love
around us and how we as individuals can touch others.
—Jessie O'Neill

CIRCLE OF LOVE No matter where I am, I am within a circle of God's love. And I find that the very truth of this statement lies in a deeper understanding of the innate spiritual nature of all people.

I have been created in love, for God, my creator, is love. I came into this world ready to love and be loved, ready to see and accept the best in myself and others.

Love lifts me up when I feel down. Love is forgiving and encourages me to forgive. Love builds and also repairs my faith. Love heals me. Love gives to me generously with no thought of return.

I live and function in a circle of God's love that is always radiating out in waves of compassion and understanding, healing and inspiration, so that I can never move beyond the blessing of its touch.

We live and function in a circle of God's love.

Day 65

——◆——

*I try to avoid looking forward or backward
and try to keep looking upward.*
—Charlotte Brontë

**DIVINE
INSPIRATION**

Today may be a day of decision for me. Whether my decisions concern myself, my loved ones, or a job situation, I take time to remember God and to let my thoughts, words, and actions be divinely inspired.

Even if the guidance I receive from God does not seem to be something I prefer, I remove my own ego from the situation. I realize that God knows what is best for me in all circumstances.

The power and wisdom of God surpass all time and space, and the solutions I seek are even now being presented to me—as a gentle urging within or as a clear plan.

So I listen to the inspiration of God, and I act with confidence and faith. My steps never falter, for I am being divinely guided to say and do what blesses all people involved.

My thoughts, words, and actions are divinely guided.

Day 66

—◆—

*Every great work, every great accomplishment,
has been brought into manifestation through holding to
the vision.—Florence Scovel Shinn*

TO MOVE MOUNTAINS A mountain of a problem can be overcome through faith in God and through use of my own God-given abilities. So whenever the problem I face seems like a mountain, I bring it down to a manageable size as I affirm my faith in God. I know that nothing is impossible for me through the power of my Creator.

With God, all things are possible. Even the seemingly impossible becomes possible when I put God first, when I trust God to show me the way. My faith in God is a confidence-booster that gives me the courage to act when action is needed and not to act when a calm presence is best.

Within me lies a vast reservoir of strength and knowledge. I face each day with faith, for divine potential is within me. My possibilities become realities through the power of God.

I have faith that moves mountains.

Day 67

—◆—

Worry a little bit every day and in a lifetime you will lose a couple of years. . . . Worry never fixes anything.—Mary Hemingway

EXPRESSION OF SPIRIT

God, when I am in need of comfort, Your loving presence fills me, relieving every longing of my heart. I am ready for whatever the day may bring.

You are always with me, God—even when I am so busy at work or at home that I may not be consciously aware of You. But then a gentle nudge from my subconscious speaks to me of Your love and grace all around me. You are the voice of compassion I hear, the encouraging smile of a friend, the words of love spoken—just what I need when I need it.

So whatever happens today, I know that You are right here with me, encouraging me and reminding me of what I may have forgotten: I can succeed. You see in me what I may not always see in myself: I am an expression of Your divine spirit. You and I are one.

You comfort me, God, with Your loving, light-filled presence.

Day 68

—◆—

Great thoughts speak only to the thoughtful mind,
but great actions speak to all mankind.
—Emily P. Bissell

BREAKING FREE When I leave my familiar surroundings for someplace new, I may feel like a stranger at first. Even though I know I have made a wise move, I may feel uncomfortable with my own excitement over something wonderful happening.

And so it goes when I move past the familiar, yet negative, habits from which I am breaking free. This is new for me and exciting, yet it is such a change. So I give myself a chance for a breakthrough by living with the newness for a while.

While I am settling in with this achievement or change, I talk it over with my Creator. I want to be so aware of divine guidance, strength, and peace that I recognize and accept each whisper of an idea about them all and then incorporate these divine ideas in my life and living.

Aware of God, I am aware of my freedom.

Day 69

—◆—

When I pray, I give thanks to God.
Every day I get up and I thank God that I'm alive.
—Phyllis Diller

ON THE HORIZON If I were basing my judgment on how the horizon looks, I would believe the surface of the Earth ends within a few miles of where I stand. Yet basing my judgment on experience, I know that the world and the glory of God's creation do continue beyond my point of view.

Whenever appearances seem bleak and I start to become concerned about my prosperity, I remember that there are blessings beyond the horizon. From my own experience and through my faith, I know that God is constantly supplying me with whatever I need. Whether in my relationships, job, or finances, I know there is so much more beyond what seems to be, for God is my provider.

So I look beyond appearances. I have strength of mind and a wisdom I have cultivated throughout a lifetime—a lifetime in which God has provided for me.

God is my life and provides my every blessing.

Day 70

—◆—

Beloved,

I have never condemned you and I never will condemn you, My child. Because My love for you is so great, I have allowed you to learn from your own life experiences. I watched you turn seeming errors into lessons and supported you as you discovered just how much you are capable of doing. All the while, I guided you as you continued your life's journey.

Through all experiences, draw upon your faith in Me and let My presence nourish you. In moments of sweet surrender, you will learn the meaning of true love and all that it entails. If a mountain stands in your way, you can climb it. If a problem weighs heavily upon your mind, you can solve it. With My help, you can do all things. And with your faith in Me, you will do them.

You will learn throughout your life and draw closer to Me each day. I am your God, and I can make your dreams a reality.

"You will say to this mountain, 'Move from here to there,' and it will move."
—Matthew 17:20

Day 71

— ◆ —

Live daily in the awareness of God's presence
in you, as you. This is true Oneness.
—Sue Sikking

SPIRITUAL ONENESS
Whenever I feel uncertain or anxious about some challenge, I reassure myself with words of encouragement such as these: "God and I will handle this challenge together!"

There is no need to worry about problems or to be afraid to face them—worry and fret will never solve any problem. So with strength of spirit, I stop hiding from circumstances or lashing out at them. I face the challenge with courage and conviction born of faith and fueled by God's love for me.

I affirm: "The past has no power over me. My true reality lies within my spiritual oneness with God. Nothing can keep me from realizing this truth."

God and I are one, and I can never be separated from the love, understanding, and peace of God.

I am one with the love, understanding, and peace of God.

Day 72

---◆---

When one person would help another through prayer,
what he really does is to take him by the hand . . . and
help him to set his feet upon the path that leads to his own
divine source.—Vera Dawson Tait

GREATEST GIFT
I give thanks for you today—for the love which you share with me, for the joy which you bring to my life.

I bless you in my prayers this day and every day. I find such comfort in knowing that God's spirit within you is constantly protecting and guiding you—so much more efficiently and effectively than I myself or anyone else is capable of doing.

I bless you with a gift today—the gift of my prayers for your health and safety, for your happiness and success. Although God's love cannot be bought or packaged, it is the greatest gift I could possibly share with you. I love you and know that the spirit of God is the supreme caregiver. I gently release you into God's care and keeping.

In prayer, I give thanks to God for you.

Day 73

*We rise on the wings of prayer into a realm of joy,
and we retain the beauty of the experience in every act
of our lives.—May Rowland*

BEING PREPARED

When I am thinking about the activities of the day ahead, do I always remember to include God in my plans? Spending time with God in prayer is vital to the success of any venture. Prayer is the first step in ensuring that my plans will go smoothly and that even if they don't, I will be okay and do well.

I begin my prayer time by finding a quiet space or place and tuning out any distractions. I let go of the worries of the moment and concentrate fully on God.

Just a few moments with God refresh me and prepare me for what is to come. I feel more in tune with the order of the universe and more prepared to handle whatever comes my way.

Aware of God, I am also aware of God's wisdom and love. I am ready for some great achievements!

God prepares me for great achievements.

Day 74

———◆———

We are all in mind related to that great creative spirit that infuses its life into our minds and bodies when we turn our attention to it.—Connie Fillmore Bazzy

GOD'S FAMILY

God's spirit lives in me and in every person on Earth. The divine presence within each of us connects us one with another, so we truly are the family of God that spans the globe.

God is love, and every person on Earth is a member of the universal family of love and goodwill. Whether I am aware of it or not, everything I say and do has an impact on other people. So I do my best to bring a loving attitude to my conversations and activities.

What a blessing it is to know that wherever I go, I am in the company of family members! We may have our differences—all families do—but we are divinely connected, so it is possible for us to overcome even the greatest of challenges.

I am a member of God's universal family of love.

Day 75

—◆—

Invest in the human soul. Who knows,
it might be a diamond in the rough.
—Mary McLeod Bethune

 **MOVING FORWARD**   If I have been holding back forgiveness toward someone, I now release it in silent thought and feel a surge of relief:

"Wherever you are, I forgive you. I let go the past and envision us both free to live our lives without regrets or recriminations.

"You are special to me because of who you are—a child of God capable of being God's love in expression. I bless you in my prayers. Even if I never see you again, I will think of you often and trust that you are living a life of joy and peace.

"And if I see you tomorrow, know that I am filled with great happiness—happiness at seeing you again and happiness for each new opportunity to begin again. The past is behind us, and we are moving forward to a bright new future."

With love in my heart, I can and do forgive.

Day 76

—◆—

*My heart is singing for joy this morning!
A miracle has happened! The light of
understanding has shone upon my little pupil's mind,
and behold, all things are changed!—Anne Sullivan*

HARMONY

Listen closely—can you hear the beautiful melody being sung by different people as they work together in peace and love?

Minute by minute, hour by hour, day by day, loving people around the world are joining in the chorus of heartfelt thoughts and prayers for world peace, with each person contributing his or her own individual notes of joy to this worldwide song of peace.

I do my part, too. Every day I look for ways to promote harmony in my own environment. I am kind and loving even when others may not be. But most important of all, I spend time with God in prayer. Because I am in tune with God, I am in harmony with the universe.

**I am in tune with God and in harmony
with the universe.**

Day 77

—◆—

Beloved,

Know at all times that you have the strength of My spirit within you. I see that strength moving within you and out from you as life and health, love and compassion.

Know, also, that each time you pray for others, you are letting My presence within you be expressed by you. Every positive thought about yourself or another is a prayer, an expression of your faith in My presence within you, within others, and within the world.

You and I and everything else that I have created share a divine connection. There is a steady beat of life resounding through all creation. This beat proclaims My life and love within all there is or ever will be.

My strength is yours. My joy is yours. My all is yours, for you are My beloved.

"I am Gabriel. I stand in the presence of God, and I have been sent to speak to you and to bring you this good news."
—Luke 1:19

Day 78

—◆—

*Joy is a light that fills you with hope
and faith and love.*
—Adela Rogers St. Johns

**CREATED
IN JOY**
I may feel no joy in being caught in rush hour traffic. But if I happen to turn on the car radio and hear a resounding chorus of Beethoven's "Ode to Joy," I can't help but be filled with feelings of gladness.

What has happened? The joy of one of the world's greatest composers has reached across more than a century of time to strike a chord of joy within me.

Once the traffic begins to move, I feel lighthearted and in no need to hurry. So I let the driver next to me change lanes and get in front of me. Yes, I am being the joy of God I was created to be.

The joy that God created Beethoven to express is the same joy I was created to express. I may not compose a work of art, but a simple act of kindness can sound a note of joy within others.

God has created me in joy and created me to express joy.

Day 79
—◆—

I touch the future. I teach.
—Christa McAuliffe

BEING A BLESSING   We are all blessed with a responsibility—caring about and loving all God's creations. And part of this responsibility may include being a parent or taking on the role of a parent.

Children are the world's future, and I do my best to ensure that the children in my life receive the guidance and love they need. If circumstances require that I become a caregiver for my parents, I do so with faith and acceptance that all things are in divine order.

God's creations in nature rely on people to act responsibly toward them, too, so that they can thrive in a peaceful environment. So I act with care to bless the environment of the world.

At all times, I am a nurturing, loving person, acting in divinely guided ways.

I am a nurturing, loving person.

DAILY WORD FOR WOMEN

Day 80

— ◆ —

Your body is a place where God lives.
It also is the home of your soul.
—Mary-Alice Jafolla

WHOLE AND HOLY

This is a day of great expectation—yet my expectation is not of what I can do but of what God can do through me and others. Every prayer I pray is a vital link that connects my expectations with the reality of God's presence in every moment of this day:

"God, thank You for always being with me. In Your presence, I know how it feels to be whole and holy. I know how it feels to have a clear mind, a healthy body, and a divine spirit. I know how it feels to live a spiritually enriched life."

An awareness of God goes before me, paving my way with wisdom, patience, love, and understanding. My appreciation for God resounds throughout my being as love that soothes my soul and reaches out to others in absolute acceptance.

I am a whole and holy being—mind, body, and spirit.

Day 81

—◆—

*This communion is an attitude of mind and heart
that lifts the individual into a wonderful sense of oneness
with God.—Myrtle Fillmore*

**QUIET
OF
PRAYER**

In the quiet of prayer, I am embraced by God. In that sacred embrace, I know more of God as divine love, life, and wisdom. I know God in a way that leaves no room for doubt.

In the quiet of prayer, I ask to see the world through loving, faith-filled eyes. I share the longings of my heart and soul. God answers by giving me the understanding I need to live a life of love and faith.

In the quiet of prayer, I bless myself and the family of God throughout this lush, beautiful planet we call home. I pray that the needs of all people are being met, that each person is becoming more aware of the important contribution he or she is making to the world.

**In the quiet of prayer, I seek God
and God answers.**

Day 82
—◆—

*Let us become little children in expectancy and learn
to dream dreams and have visions of beauty and wonder
beyond all we have seen or read about.—Sue Sikking*

**BEAUTY
OF SPIRIT**
There is a beauty that surpasses all others, a beauty of spirit that shines forth from me with every act of kindness, every prayer for another, every recognition of the divine spirit that unites us all.

In spirit, age and gender do not matter. Neither do experiences from the past or present. Everyone has an inner beauty, and it is expressed in a language of the soul that overcomes all barriers to uplift and inspire, to communicate and comfort.

Beauty of spirit is so beyond what the senses can detect that I may not have recognized it before. But now I can. I recognize myself and all others as spiritual beings, and I see the beauty of God within all of us that is always ready to shine forth.

**I look for and find the beauty of God's spirit
in every person.**

Day 83

——◆——

*What is genius but the power of
expressing a new individuality?*
—Elizabeth Barrett Browning

TRANSFORMED In order to change what is
happening to me or through me, I need
to take a closer look at what is
happening within me. My attitudes,
thoughts, and beliefs are what eventually come from
me as words and actions.

Even deeper within me is a power that will infuse
all that I think, say, and do with patience, love,
and understanding. The power of God within is the
starting point to being the loving person I desire to be in
my relationships with family and friends, and even on
the job.

What I say and do is not forced by a feeling of
responsibility, duty, or loyalty. Rather, I speak and act
from the pure and absolute joy of letting the power of
God surge through. When I let God come through, I am
transformed.

**The power of God transforms me and affects all
that I think, say, and do.**

Day 84

—◆—

Beloved,

You were created in joy to be a blessing. The beauty of your soul is a beacon of love, a beacon to others of the whole and holy beings you and they are!

You are a source of inspiration in the world! As you grow and unfold more and more each day, you will be an example for others—an example of how to live from the beauty of spirit within. My spirit is within you and within all people, and nothing is impossible for you individually or collectively with others.

Yes, you were created in joy—and joy is yours to express in abundance as you more fully realize the unlimited potential that lies within you.

"My spirit within me
earnestly seeks you."
—Isaiah 26:9

Day 85

— ◆ —

Life begets life. Energy creates energy.
It is by spending oneself that one becomes
rich.—Sarah Bernhardt

ALIVE!   What a glorious feeling it is to know that the healing, energizing life of God is surging throughout my entire body, renewing me and making me well! How wonderful it is to be alive!

So whether I am involved in a physical activity or sitting at rest, I take time to give thanks to God. I give thanks for the divine life that is present in every cell of my body, and I express my appreciation in heartfelt prayer. I am completely in awe of the physical body— a work of art created by God.

From the top of my head to the tips of my toes, I feel God's life within me! I am alive with the life of God! "Thank You, thank You, God, for this wonderful body and for the ability to understand and appreciate myself as one of Your great works!"

I am alive with the life of God!

Day 86

—◆—

What we are doing is just a drop in the ocean. But if that drop was not in the ocean, I think the ocean would be less because of that missing drop.—Mother Teresa

PART OF THE WHOLE

When I consider the wonder of God's creation—the stars, planets, animals, people, and so much more—I catch a glimpse of the variety and vastness of life.

God's world is teeming with life, even in the spots that seem barren. And supporting all the activity that is going on and coming forth is an order which never ceases to sustain and uphold.

So whenever my life seems out of order, I remember the wonder of God's creation and the order that holds it together. It may be in order for me to make adjustments in the way I think and in what I do. But as I make those adjustments, I remember that I am part of a wonderful whole that is divine order.

My life is in order because I am an intricate part of an orderly whole.

Day 87

—◆—

Only as we become completely aware that we are . . . God's child, chosen to house . . . God's presence, do we become reverent about our body and want it to be a fit place for the Spirit of God to inhabit.—Mary Katherine MacDougall

SPIRIT OF GOD

I have been given a wonderful responsibility—caring for and maintaining my body. My body is a temple of the spirit of life, and in accepting this responsibility, I am paving the way to health and peace.

In my prayer times—my quiet moments with God—I make a conscious connection with the presence of God. I am infused with healing energy. Every cell and muscle in my body is alive and responsive to the divine life that lives in me.

I bless my mind and body for the tremendous work they perform. My mind, body, and spirit are in perfect order, which I gain through my awareness of God.

The spirit of God lives within me—now and always.

Day 88

—◆—

*Your greatest prayer for another is the realization
that God is within . . . a loving presence . . . that heals
and guides and blesses. Feel your oneness with those
for whom you pray.—Martha Smock*

**DOING
MY PART**

When people I know need help, I
may wonder what I can do that would
help them the most. One thing I can
do any time is to pray for them, to
hold them in my thoughts and have faith that they will
be blessed:

"Dear one, I am including you in my prayers today
because I love and cherish you. In prayer, I see you as
you really are—a magnificent creation of God who is
surrounded and enfolded in divine light and love.

"God is always with you. With God, you can
overcome any challenge. You are a radiant beacon of
divine love for all the world to see.

"No other person in the world can give what you
have to give. So don't give up. Just by being you, you
are a blessing to the world!"

I bless the world by blessing others in my prayers.

Day 89

---◆---

But warm, eager, living life—to be rooted in life—to learn, to desire to know, to feel, to think, to act. This is what I want. And nothing else. That is what I must try.
—Katherine Mansfield

FREE TO BE I may feel comfortable with old habits and routines simply because they are familiar; however, I now feel it is time to change my course in life. But how do I begin?

The first step toward any change is to know that I have the freedom to change. And that freedom to change soars when I know with all my heart that I can quit any negative habit or start a life-enhancing routine.

I don't let time or circumstance dictate what I can do and when I can do it. In my freedom to be, I know that there is a way. God will show me the way when I am open to receiving it.

Through the spirit of God within me, I have the freedom to do and be my best.

With the spirit of God in me, I am free to do my best.

Day 90

—◆—

I must admit I personally measure success in terms of the contributions an individual makes to her or his fellow human beings.—Margaret Mead

KIND TO THE WORLD

I know how I feel when someone is not kind to me. So I give extra attention today to being kind, to listening with my heart and trying to be more understanding.

Giving love is my first priority. A little love and attention can make anyone feel special—and we are all special, because we are all part of God.

I do what I can to bring peace to every situation. How? By treating everyone I know with the kindness and respect they deserve. God is within every person—and that is all I need to know to be as helpful as I can be.

If my own feelings get in the way, I trust God to bring me to a new level of understanding. God's love lives in me, so I can be an ambassador of goodwill in the world.

I am kind and understanding.

THE HEALING GIFT
OF LAUGHTER
BY PHYLLIS DILLER

I didn't start out to be a comic. It just happened. I had been a mother and a housewife for 15 years and never expected to have a career of any kind except motherhood.

Yet I found that when I told a joke, I not only made others laugh, but I enjoyed myself, too! I discovered that laughter and humor are healing gifts. While we're laughing, every cell in our bodies is laughing and giving off endorphins—and healing in the process.

We can use laughter as a healing treatment. Author Norman Cousins did. He showed us what laughter can do for health when he was so ill that his doctors were unable to help him with any kind of treatment or drugs. The doctors told him he was going to die. So Norman left the hospital, checked into a hotel, and there proceeded to cure himself with laughter while watching classic comedy movies!

I have watched laughter transform people who attend my comedy routines. I hear and see how good they feel after an hour of laughing. And I get the greatest lift in the world. In fact, I'm the one who probably benefits the most!

Many comics have something in their childhood that

gives them a bent toward comedy, and one such thing is being an only child, which I am. I think I also developed comedy as a defense system for not being what I considered a great beauty.

I got in touch with my own spirituality very early in life, because my parents were the age of grandparents and many of their friends and relatives were dying. At a young age, I attended so many funerals that I started thinking about life and what it's all about. I began to question and to formulate my own ideas.

Later on, two pamphlets changed my life: *The Golden Key* and *The Mental Equivalent*. When I'm lecturing and someone says he or she is trapped in a situation, I love to tell a story from *The Mental Equivalent*—the one about a man who was thrown into a dungeon. For 20 years he lay there, never attempting to even rattle the door. If he had, he could have set himself free because, from the beginning, the door was never locked!

So often, like the man in the dungeon, we allow our own thoughts about a situation to trap us. We can free ourselves through prayer. I pray every day. When I pray, I give thanks to God. Every morning I get up and thank God that I'm alive by using this affirmation: "On this happy day, oh God, thank You for my blessings!"

Day 91

—◆—

Beloved,

Each day is a new beginning—a new opportunity for you to be My love in expression as acceptance and kindness in the world and toward the world.

My love is the source of your compassionate attitude toward others. Being aware of My spirit within you is a great starting point in your being understanding of others—every day.

Each and every person—including you—is an integral part of My universal plan. Each and every person—including you—is designed to live life joyously and with the freedom of spirit that only I can give.

I love you, sweet child. Now go forth and be My love in expression in every circumstance in which you are a part.

"Behold, the kingdom of God
is in the midst of you."
—Luke 17:21

Day 92

♦

*Our visions begin
with our desires.
—Audre Lorde*

NEW VISION

If I had the opportunity to observe a familiar object under a microscope, I would find that the more I increased the magnification, the less recognizable the object would be.

The same holds true for any situation in my life that is still in the process of being resolved. If I focus only on the problem, I will be drawn closer to it. In an attempt to analyze it, I can become so completely involved that my perception is distorted.

Instead, I focus on God and God's overall plan. I keep an open mind and heart. When I do, I can look objectively with a new vision—with God's vision of truth and order.

As I look with fresh eyes and a better perspective, I am able to see that God is, indeed, in charge and that all is coming together according to a divine plan.

**God is opening my eyes to all the possibilities
that this day brings.**

Day 93

—◆—

Relaxation is not inaction. It is perfect poise in Spirit that enables one to crest the waves of life composed, serene, joyous, and unafraid.—Clara Palmer

R E S T Even when I seem to get plenty of sleep, I may sometimes feel tired. I know that there is more to rest than just letting my body be inactive; I need to refresh my soul as well. Prayer is the refresher of the soul.

Knowing that God is here with me, I can relax and let God's spirit move through me to clear away all thoughts of concern or fear. Although I may shut the outer door to the world when I sleep, I leave the inner door open to the sanctuary of my soul.

God blesses me while I sleep. The life of God breathes through me. Divine order establishes and maintains the beat of my heart and the circulation within my bloodstream. When I awaken, I feel refreshed, because God has given me complete rest.

The spirit of God gives me complete rest.
I am refreshed.

Day 94
—◆—

I want to be all that I am capable
of becoming.
—Katherine Mansfield

GOD-GIVEN POTENTIAL

When an acorn grows into a towering tree or a cygnet into a graceful swan, it is fulfilling its potential. This growth does not happen because the seedling or cygnet deliberately set its own plan into action; it is living out a divine plan.

I, too, follow a divine plan by following the guidance I receive from God in order to fulfill my potential. My life is in a constant state of change and adaptation, and my mind is alert and receptive to the God-given potential that lies within me, waiting to be expressed.

Every person, animal, and plant created by God has been given potential. And just as the acorn becomes the tree or the cygnet the swan, I change from day to day, increasing my awareness of God and realizing that I am living out a divine plan and fulfilling my potential.

I am fulfilling my God-given potential.

Day 95

——◆——

I believe music is the breath of God.
I think it's a healer.
—Naomi Judd

RADIANT EXPRESSION

God created me to express life, and that is what I do when I realize that divine life is at the very core of my being. Life—healing life—surges from every atom of my body. I am alive with the life of God, and I feel energized and strong. I am a radiant expression of God!

Any concern dissolves quickly when I understand that God intended me to live my life fully. God formed my body to express health and wholeness, to work efficiently throughout an entire lifetime. So I do not accept any belief that my body is less than what God created it to be.

Every hour of every day, I am becoming more of what I was created to be. Thank God, I am a radiant expression of divine life!

The life of God surges through my body, healing me.

Day 96

——◆——

In youth we learn;
in age we understand.
—*Marie Ebner-Eschenbach*

JOURNEY WITH GOD

When I view my life as a journey, I can look back with new understanding. Yes, those turns and detours that at one time seemed so unnecessary actually moved me to where I need to be today. Looking forward, I know the road I take today leads me to a new tomorrow.

Sometimes I make the choice to blaze a new trail; sometimes I choose to stay on a well-worn path. But no matter which route I choose, I always make each decision based on divine guidance. Mine is a journey with God, a journey of living in the wonder of every new scene and celebrating the joy of every new discovery.

I give thanks for the people who walk beside me, and I bless others as we go our separate ways. Life is a glorious journey as I walk in faith with God.

My life is a journey with God.

Day 97

— ◆ —

We all live in suspense, from day to day,
from hour to hour; in other words, we are the hero
of our own story.—Mary McCarthy

CREATING MY DAY

What kind of day am I helping to create? It is true that, with my thoughts, words, and activities, I help create the kind of day I experience and share.

For instance, I may think of how it feels to have no other thought than that of enjoying the life which God has given me. Now I hold on to that feeling for just a moment and see myself enjoying the whole day. By doing so, I am in fact creating my day with an attitude of expectancy and jubilation.

As I envision myself meeting people and working with them, I see a smile on my face. And I can imagine that they are smiling back at me. I let a feeling of assurance help create an atmosphere of confidence and trust.

I enjoy the gift of life that God has given me.

Day 98

———◆———

Beloved,

The life you lead may take you in many different directions. Only I know what the future will hold, so release your worries and concerns to Me and enjoy each day for the beauty that it holds.

Consider the journey that has brought you to this point. Looking back, can you now see order where there appeared to be chaos? Are you now able to recognize that you were never alone—that I was with you all the while?

These things that I tell you are true. You are in My care now, and I will always care for you. I am closer than the air you breathe, more powerful than any force known on Earth, and gentler than the flutter of butterfly wings.

I will love and care for you forever, for we are forever one.

"For I, the Lord your God,
hold your right hand."
—Isaiah 41:13

Day 99

—◆—

Tears may be dried up,
but the heart—never.
—Marguerite de Valois

PEACEFUL
One major challenge or several minor challenges may leave me feeling as if I am carrying a greater load than I am able to bear. Yet my load will disappear and concern will be forgotten when I know with all my being that God in me is my strength, wisdom, and peace.

In a quiet moment of prayer, I reflect on this truth: God in me is my strength. As I let the idea of inner strength grow within me, I feel myself becoming stronger.

If today is a day of decision, I calm myself by knowing that God in me is all the wisdom I could ever need. My decisions are based on divine guidance.

I stop myself from being caught up in the whirl of seeming confusion around me by declaring that God in me is my peace. I am peaceful.

God in me is my strength, my wisdom, and my peace.

Day 100

—◆—

Age is something that doesn't matter,
unless you are a cheese.
—Billie Burke

ENERGIZED Positive words are the beginning to an enthusiastic outlook for all that life has to offer. So each day I begin by affirming "I am alive and enthusiastic about life!" Just saying these words gives me new energy and an extra boost to start my day.

I am alive! I am alive with the life of God, and I feel this life pulsating throughout my entire body. I feel strong and capable.

I am alert! My mind is fresh, and I think clearly about what to do next. I am filled with new ideas as I open my mind to God.

I am enthusiastic about life and ready for the golden opportunities that await me this day! God is always with me, preparing me for new and exciting adventures in living. I look forward to all the possibilities!

I am alive and enthusiastic about life!

Day 101

$\longrightarrow\blacklozenge\longrightarrow$

Our purpose is to love one another, to love
those around us, to love ourselves. Love, love, love.
—Sophy Burnham

CHANNELS OF BLESSINGS   One of the quickest ways to forget what I think I need is to give thanks for the blessings I already have. So I dedicate today as a day for counting my blessings, for giving thanks for my life and for all life.

I thank God for my family and friends, and for all people who support me and encourage me to be all that I am capable of being. They uplift me and give me love and understanding because they are, in reality, channels of God's blessings.

Above all else, I thank God for being such a loving Creator. God has made a beautiful world that provides me with all the resources I will ever need to live prosperously.

God is blessing me now.

Day 102

◆

For me, there is no separation between a spiritual life, a secular life, a life engaged. It is seeing the world whole, even holy.—Terry Tempest Williams

PRAYER OF THE SOUL
At times I have asked God for the things I thought I needed in order to be happy or fulfilled, and God has always listened to me.

Time after time, I came away from my prayer so satisfied that I forgot what I thought I needed. What I had received was a satisfaction of the soul that built upon itself each time I prayed, each time I made a conscious connection with Spirit Divine.

I now realize that the purpose of my prayer time is not to get things or fix situations. In prayer, I sit in silence with God and listen, and I talk as God listens. There is no reward that is greater, no gift that is of more value than knowing God.

God, with every prayer, I realize more
of You within me and around me.

Day 103

——◆——

*I don't think there is anything as wonderful in life
as being able to help someone else. But believe me,
it's through the grace of God that I'm able to do it.*
—*Betty Ford*

**TURNING
POINT**
I may have heard that people
with addictions or negative habits
must hit bottom before they can rise
to the top when dealing with their
emotions or habits.

But I know in my own heart and mind that this is
not always true. I give thanks to God that my turning
points are not born of desperation; they come from my
aspirations.

If something in my life needs to change, then the
spirit of God within will guide me to do just that. My
turning points may come when I feel guided to change
my place of employment, to work on a negative habit,
or to become part of a lasting, loving relationship. As I
listen to divine Spirit, I am at peace.

Spirit Divine guides me through any changes I make.

Day 104

— ◆ —

*The more I understand about my own spirituality
and the spirituality of others, the more I struggle
to obtain yet more knowledge.—Betty Eadie*

**GOD IN
ACTION**

What is the grace of God if it is not the love of God in action?

Grace is the gentle, silent urging that lifts me when I feel down, assures me that I am not alone at any time, and gives me strength when I need it most.

Grace instills me with the motivation to try something new and gives me the courage to not limit the results with my expectations—of failure or success.

The love of God washes over me, healing all superficial or deep-seated hurts. And I emerge a healthy and whole person, ready to live the life and share the love that God has so generously given me.

The grace of God uplifts, heals, and strengthens me.

Day 105

———◆———

Beloved,

Out of my unconditional love for all, I have created a world in which no two people are exactly alike. Yet all people are equally cherished by Me— just as *you* are, My beloved.

As you interact with others, think of Me. Act as you know I would act toward you. Speak words of love and compassion—just as I do to you. Each of My creations is worthy of being loved and appreciated.

As you look at those who hold a special place in your heart, think of what blessings they have shared with you. Then think of what a blessing you are to them.

In all your conversations, let your words be from love. In any situation, turn to Me for guidance. Make your life a prayer, and let your actions speak of your faith in Me and love for all. In all ways and at all times, live in peace.

"Live in harmony with one another."
—Romans 12:16

Day 106

—◆—

People are like stained glass windows. They sparkle and shine when the sun is out, but when the darkness sets in, their true beauty is revealed only if there is a light from within.—Elizabeth Kubler-Ross

HEALING

How can I ever take my health for granted? I never will whenever I think about and appreciate the intricate, powerful, life-supporting work my digestive system, lungs, and heart do while I am awake and asleep.

And I never wait until something seems to go wrong to bless my body with words of appreciation. The underlying message that supports those words is my recognition of the life of God in my body, life that responds to my life-affirming thoughts and words.

I go a step further by visualizing some area of my body that needs healing saturated with healing life. I imagine myself aglow with the life of God. Yes, the life of God is within me, healing and restoring me now.

I bless myself by visualizing the spirit of God radiating throughout my body.

Day 107

—◆—

*Practice the presence of God daily and think in
a positive, spiritual way, and you will be changing
and transforming your soul.—Elinor McDonald*

**BE STILL
AND
KNOW**

Most likely I would not attempt to
repair something when I was unsure
of how to fix it—not until I had first
consulted a repair manual or spoken
with an expert.

The same is true when I am working on problems
that I may be experiencing in my life; I do not take any
action without first seeking guidance from God.

In prayer, I open myself to divine direction and enter
into the inner sanctuary of my soul. In silence, I listen
to God. No audible words are spoken or needed
because God speaks a language that my heart and mind
understand.

I leave my quiet time with confidence in myself and
in what I am doing, for I have been blessed with
wisdom from God. In silence, I listen, and in that same
silence, God answers.

In silence, I listen.

Day 108

◆

Life isn't one straight line. Most of us have
to be transplanted, like a tree, before we blossom.
—Louise Nevelson

GOD KNOWS ME

If my desire is to make improvements in myself and in my life, I may become frustrated—especially if others are unable to understand where I am coming from and where I want to go. However, there is always one who knows and understands.

God knows me better than any person can and even better than I know myself. So I let go of doubt and fear. God sees my life from a bigger perspective and gently guides me along my way.

I release the past and any worries that have been clouding my vision. I look at the world with spiritual vision, which is a perception inspired by God.

God will never fail me. Because I know this is true, I have all the peace and understanding I could ever possibly need.

God is gently guiding me along my way.

Day 109

—◆—

*It is the inner peace within ourselves
that is our power against every adversary.
—Sue Sikking*

SANCTUARY OF PEACE In the middle of a crisis, I may become caught up in trying to think of some way—any way—out of it. Yet when I pause for a moment and take a deep breath, I begin to understand that the way to peace is not getting out of a situation; it is going within to my own internal center of peace.

God's spirit within me welcomes me to a place of absolute peace and unconditional love. I feel all pressure and stress melt away. Aware of the presence of God, I am also aware that the life of God strengthens me and the love of God comforts me. And most important, the peace of God flows through me.

No matter where I am or what I am going through, I have a sanctuary of peace where I can withdraw to and be refreshed. Inner peace radiates out into all that I do.

**Aware of the peace of God within me,
I bring peacefulness to all that I do.**

Day 110

—◆—

*The greater part of our happiness or misery
depends on our dispositions and not our circumstances.*
—Martha Washington

BEACON OF LIGHT I would never think of stumbling around in a darkened room when I know I can have light by flipping on a light switch. So why would I ever wander in the dark of confusion when I can turn to God for understanding?

God is the light of pure understanding that shines within me at all times. If I feel I am in the dark, I need to open the windows of my soul to the light of God.

And God immediately fills me with the light of love and peace. At peace, I am open to the creative ideas God has for me.

When I act on the divine ideas I receive, I truly am a beacon of God's light in the world. And by letting my light shine, I am letting God bless and encourage others through me.

**God's light of understanding
shines from within me.**

Day 111

—◆—

Harmony within brings
harmony without.
—Rebecca Clark

I BELIEVE

I may have noticed that when I feel upset on the inside, the world around me seems to be in confusion, too. And the opposite is true as well—when I feel calm and at peace with myself, the world takes on a calmer look and feel.

Yet, how do I remain at peace in a world where chaos can occur, where the newsworthy items are reports of turmoil and strife between people and nations? The way is through faith in God.

I believe in God and in the power of God's love. I believe that I can live from the love of God within me. My faith is strong, so I can be at peace. I believe that I can make a difference in the world. I believe that each individual can make a difference. Then the world will be a peace-filled reflection of the harmony within all people.

I believe in God, and I believe that my world
is a reflection of the harmony I feel within.

Day 112

————◆————

Beloved,

Be still. Be still, and know that I have created you. Know that I am your constant companion, and that I love you.

Be still, and know that you are always in My care. Wherever you may be, I am there also, and I will keep you safe.

Be still, and know that I will guide you to the highest points of exhilaration in your life's journey. I feel your joy as My own.

Be still, and know that I am the one Power in the universe. I created the heavens and the earth to supply your every need.

Be still, and know that whenever you need reassurance, I will comfort you and give you understanding. Know deep in your heart that you can rely on Me in every situation. There is nothing that I could not or would not do for you and through you, My beloved.

"Be still, and know that I am God!"
—Psalm 46:10

Day 113

—◆—

Faith is the spiritual side
of hope.
—Martha Smock

THE WAY
OF FAITH
Whenever I meet a roadblock as I travel, I know there is a good reason for that obstacle to be there at that place and time. I also know there is another way to my destination.

And I know that—in all matters—faith is the way around obstacles and challenges. As I use my faith in God, I tap into the creativity and resourcefulness God has already given me. Spirit helps me find a way past any obstacle.

Spirit moves through me as the wisdom and strength to do what I need to do. In touch with God, I realize unlimited potential. My goals are attainable, new ideas flood my mind, and I am guided to the right solutions.

I welcome each day with joy and expectation, for I am lifted in spirit by my belief in the power of God to see me through.

With faith in God, there is no limit to
the wonder-filled possibilities I can experience.

Day 114

—◆—

No one need walk in darkness,
for within each of us is God's own Spirit.
—Marion R. Brown

GOD SUSTAINS ME

Blessed Creator, I rest in the assurance of Your presence. From the moment I was born, You have been my provider and my sustainer, and You will continue to bless me through all eternity. So I do not waste time or effort on fearing what lies ahead. Through Your grace and love, I am comforted.

God, with Your wisdom guiding me, I know that every step I take will be a forward one—a leap in spiritual awareness and understanding. And I know that I can never make a wrong move with Your intelligence encouraging me onward to the new opportunities that lie ahead.

I listen as You speak to me in quiet moments of prayer and contemplation. I have faith that my life's journey will continue forward because You are guiding my way.

> God, I feel the assurance of Your presence
> as divine guidance and encouragement.

DAILY WORD FOR WOMEN

Day 115

—◆—

*Those who contemplate the beauty of the earth
find reserves of strength that will endure as long
as life lasts.—Rachel Carson*

AMAZING WORLD

I live in a truly amazing world, an awe-inspiring world of beauty and order and peace. And the same beauty, order, and peace in the physical world are within me—within all—as creative thoughts and compassionate feelings. So I appreciate the beauty of nature as it unfolds, and I also appreciate the beauty within me and within every one of God's creations.

I appreciate the glorious hues of the sun as it rises each day, and I am reminded of the magnificent light that shines from me when I express love and understanding.

I appreciate the beauty of a rose as it slowly opens its petals, and I also appreciate the beauty of my own soul as it blooms in an ever-unfolding awareness of God.

**The beauty of nature reminds me of the inner beauty
of all people.**

Day 116

Apparent failure may hold in its rough shell the germs of a success that will blossom in time, and bear fruit throughout eternity.—Frances Watkins Harper

THIS IS THE DAY! When I experience an undeniable feeling that today is a green-light day for beginning something new, I know to go with what God is guiding me to do.

As I allow an expectancy about ending some negative habit or starting a positive one to grow within me, I invite the power of God to move into my thoughts and guide me to take action.

I listen in the quiet of my prayer time for a word or phrase that offers the first step to a new me. Even in a time of busy activity, I may suddenly know from an inner urging that there is a better way to do something. I am not struggling to overcome; I am a participant in a divine relationship that satisfies and fulfills me.

This is a day of new beginnings.

Day 117

— ◆ —

There are no mistakes . . . all events
are blessings given to us to learn from.
—Elizabeth Kubler-Ross

BLESSING OF FORGIVENESS In order to have absolute peace and harmony within my own circle of friends and family, I am forgiving.

Today I do my mental "spring cleaning" and clear my mind of any hurtful memories I might be storing. I remove the clutter of negative thoughts and leave plenty of room for positive, productive thinking.

As I forgive myself first—for any judgment or error I might have made in the past—I free myself to do better now and to do even better in the future.

Right now I forgive others for any hurtful actions, intended or unintended. I free them to do better also. The peace and harmony that begin within me now spread out to my family, my community, and beyond.

I bless myself by forgiving myself and others.

Day 118

—◆—

Prayer begins where
human capacity ends.
—Marian Anderson

GREATER
AWARENESS

God, I have crossed over an important threshold in my understanding of prayer. I believe that every thought I think about You, every word I speak that is in oneness with Your spirit is a prayer.

At times, my greatest sense of Your presence may be while I am with others in a place of worship. But it can also be in a solitary walk through a natural cathedral of woods or in the midst of a song that rises from the depths of my soul.

One thing I do know, God, is that You are always with me. And that realization of Your presence becomes so vivid, so comforting when I pray—however I choose to pray. My every prayer is to thank You and to remind myself that You are always with me.

In prayer, I realize a greater awareness of God.

Day 119

—◆—

Beloved,

Wherever you may go, I am there. Whatever you may be experiencing, I am there also!

Look around you and enjoy all that I have created to help you and others along the way. When you place your trust in Me, you will discover that miracles are unfolding all around you—and one is the miracle that you are.

You have faith that moves mountains. Through this faith, you can accomplish whatever you desire to accomplish. You are capable of forgiving and releasing whatever is in your way.

Lean on Me, and I will give you the courage and strength to step forth into a greater awareness of all that you are and all that you are capable of being. You are My precious creation, and I love you!

"Truly I tell you, if you have faith and do not doubt, not only will you do what has been done to the fig tree, but even if you say to this mountain, 'Be lifted up and thrown into the sea,' it will be done."
—Matthew 21:21

Day 120

—◆—

*It is only by adding the gifts of everyone that
the whole picture can be seen.*
—Connie Fillmore Bazzy

BECOMING MORE

Because there is only one of me, there is no one else who can give to the world what I have to give.

Every experience of my life has led me to this point, for every moment in life is a learning experience. So I am patient and kind with myself because I am learning something new each day. I am doing the best I know how to do today, but my best can always become better!

As I learn to let the spirit of God shine brightly in and through all my actions, I am being a light of God in my world. And I realize that in being true to the spirit of God within me, I am becoming more and more the creation I was created to be.

**Each day, I am becoming more and more
the magnificent creation God created me to be.**

THE POWER OF WORDS

BY MARY-ALICE JAFOLLA

I was nine years old, lying in a snowdrift, crying. The school bully had pummeled me with hard-packed "ice balls" as I tried to run home. Suddenly, I remembered an awful name some of my schoolmates called him behind his back, and in my desperation, I yelled it at him. The derogatory name cut through the icy air like a steel blade. The boy dropped the snowballs, began to cry, and quickly ran away.

That night was a landmark event in my life, for I was stunned by the capacity of words to hurt others. I slept little, and could hardly wait for daybreak, when I would go to school, find the boy, and apologize for causing him pain.

I did find him and I did apologize. The experience gave my life a direction from which I have never wavered. I promised myself then that I would never knowingly hurt another person with my words.

Oh—the bully? He never again harassed another classmate. In time, he became a well-loved leader, and went on to become a state senator! True story, I promise.

Day 121

—◆—

Pets so beautifully demonstrate unconditional,
uncritical love. They take us as we are,
for what's inside us.—Betty White

GOD BLESS ANIMALS Whether or not I have a pet of my own, I value the role pets fulfill as beloved companions in the lives of many people.

In touch with divine love within me, I am kind to all God's creatures. And I do all that I can to ensure that the nurturing environments which are necessary for their development remain intact.

I value all animals and what they contribute to my life and the lives of others. The love they provide is pure and unconditional. Each wag of a dog's tail, each purr of the cat is born of love and given without thought of return. So for the animal friends in the world and the animal companions in my own life, I say, "God, bless all animals, and thank You for the opportunity to share my life and my world with them."

Thank You, God, for all animal friends and companions.

Day 122

—◆—

God can make you anything you want to be,
but you have to put everything in his hands.
—Mahalia Jackson

GOD'S CREATION If ever I feel down about myself—what I have done or not done—I simply stop judging myself harshly and start thinking instead about what God can do through me.

I am a unique creation of the Creator of all there is and all there will ever be. Because I love and revere my Creator, how could I do anything less than love and revere myself? Instead of thinking about my mistakes, I think of how much I can accomplish because I am willing to let God help me.

Great and wonderful possibilities open up to me when I think the best about myself and see the best in myself. This kind of thought or vision frees me to be creative. And I think of and look at others with the same openness. I have love and reverence for them because they, too, are God's creations of life.

Thank You, God, for a whole world of possibilities that are open to me.

Day 123

—◆—

People see God every day, they just
don't recognize Him.
—Pearl Bailey

A L E R T

God never withholds guidance nor reserves it only for times of challenge. I give thanks that God is continually guiding me and keeping me alert to all the blessings around me: "God, when I hear a bird singing a song, I remember that this is a day for me, too, to experience fully and enjoy completely. Thank You for reminding me that I have joy to express.

"When I see a flower in full bloom, showing the beauty, texture, and life that was once contained in a tiny seed, I hear You telling me that there is also wonder within me waiting to be expressed.

"When there seems to be no way out of trouble or doubt, I give my attention to You and discover wisdom within that is more powerful than anyone or anything I can ever come up against. Yes, Your guidance leads me to great discoveries and fulfillment."

I am alert to every sign, sound,
and feeling of God's guidance.

Day 124

—◆—

*You can give the gift of peace through your loving
and harmonious attitudes and actions.*
—Martha Smock

SERENITY If I could actually feel the effects of
my thoughts on my body, I would
probably be amazed. I would feel
peaceful, quiet thoughts relax my
blood vessels so that my whole body would be
nourished continually and fully.

If I could actually feel how the positive words I speak
affect me physically, I might experience a stimulating
energy caressing the very cells of my body.

Yet, how do I think peaceful, refreshing thoughts
when I am in a crisis? How do I speak calmly when I
am under pressure? I can do both by relying on the
spirit of God within me to be the source of serenity in
my thoughts and in my words. I may not always be
aware of just how much inner peace blesses my body,
but it does. With each peaceful thought and word, the
blessing of serenity occurs.

**My peaceful thoughts and serene words
bless my body.**

Day 125

◆

The body is healed only as
the thought is healed.
—Connie Fillmore Bazzy

CELEBRATE LIFE — I am filled with the healing life of God. Divine life flows through every cell, organ, and tissue of my body.

So whenever I am feeling less than whole and well, I focus my attention on the spirit of God within. I release any body tension that might interfere with the smooth flow of healing life. As I continue to relax, I envision healing taking place in the very spot or area that needs it the most. I release all concern and know that God is doing a healing work in me.

Whenever a friend or family member needs a healing, I hold an image of him or her, smiling and responding to the healing life of God. Life—sweet, healing life—is within us. I celebrate and give thanks for God's healing life, and I know that my loved ones and I are whole and well.

I celebrate and give thanks for God's healing life.

Day 126

——◆——

Beloved,

Every day you are becoming more aware of Me, and every day you are being blessed as you learn to live from My spirit within you.

You are My creation of life, so never forget that I am but a thought away as you embark on the new adventures that each day brings.

We are one because we are united through a spiritual connection that can never be broken. Aware of our divine connection, you are alert to all the blessings that come your way. With serenity and poise, you look for the good that is yours and you accept it.

Every moment of life gives reason for a celebration, for every moment is a time in which the splendor of My spirit is unfolding from within you!

"Let your light shine before others, so that they may . . . give glory to your Father."
—Matthew 5:16

Day 127

---◆---

*If I had one wish for my children, it would be
that each of them would reach for goals that have meaning
for them as individuals.—Lillian Carter*

GRADUATION

Graduation is a time of reaching one goal only to move on to another goal. It is a time of change, anticipation, and often apprehension.

Throughout life, I graduate from one goal to another. At times, I may experience the same emotions of anticipation and apprehension when making important decisions or initiating changes in my life—especially concerning family and career.

However, I have graduated from feeling fear and doubt to feeling confident and serene knowing that I am living in God's world. I do not fear what the future may hold or worry that I have made a wrong decision. I achieve such confidence and serenity by turning to God in prayer and listening to the thoughts that reveal themselves to me. I feel at peace about the past and totally prepared for both the present and the future.

**I am confident and serene, knowing that I
am living in God's glorious world.**

Day 128

—◆—

Imagination is the highest kite
that one can fly.
—Lauren Bacall

IMAGINE Do I dream of a world where all people love and care for each other? Do I long for a time when I can turn on a radio or television and hear only news about the kind things people are doing for each other?

Well, I can be more than just a dreamer—I can also be a doer! Yes, I can imagine a world filled with harmony and love, and more than that, I know that the dream can be a reality.

I speak kind words to my friends and family. I extend loving thoughts to everyone—including the people of the world I might never meet. And if someone should attempt to frustrate my peacemaking efforts with unkind words or actions, I will respond in peace. I continue on with my goal, knowing that with God, harmony in the world is possible. Imagining that world of peace is one step forward in making it a reality.

I am more than a dreamer—I am also a doer!

Day 129

—◆—

From the moment we arrived on Earth,
we were meant to live more lovingly, purposefully,
and simply.—Susan Skog

THE
GLORY
OF SPIRIT

There is outstanding beauty in each season, and spring fairly shouts, "Look at the promise that was hidden by winter, which I am now revealing!" All this promise was once a work in progress—each blade of grass, each splash of color was taking form within the soil until the warmth of the sun drew it out.

And I, too, am a work in progress. There is promise hidden within me. God has given me all that I need in order to grow and achieve. I do my part by knowing that there is more in me than might currently be evident. I know that God will never give up on me, so I do not give up on myself.

I am a work in progress, and every day is a season of promise for me—a time to reveal the inner glory of God through what I think, do, and say.

I am a work in progress, revealing the inner glory of spirit.

Day 130

◆

Our spirituality is our opening to one another
as whole human beings, each different and precious,
and our exploring how we can truly learn to love.
—Jean Grasso Fitzpatrick

WE ARE ONE

No matter how different people may look on the outside, each person has something within that is universally inherent in all: God's loving spirit.

The spirit of God that is within me and within every other person on Earth unites us in a bond of spirit and soul. Through the spirit of God, I am one with all people.

There is no challenge that I cannot overcome. I help to create a beautiful symphony of love and goodwill that resounds throughout the universe and spreads understanding.

One with God, I am one with all of God's creation. God is my source of peace, and I share that peace with the world through my loving thoughts and actions.

One with God, I am one with the world of God's creation.

Day 131

—◆—

*Focus your attention upon knowing again and again,
"God is showing me how!" You will find that . . .
good will result.—Mary L. Kupferle*

**DIVINE
SOLUTIONS**
If I had to understand how everything I use in life works, I would probably not get much done. I know that my car, computer, and oven work for me, and I use them.

I am glad I don't have to know why the sun comes up every day in order to enjoy a sunrise. I just give thanks for the spectacular beauty in the display of color and light.

I am blessed every day by the activity of God's order in the world. I am free to live my life in the order that God has created.

In all matters and all situations, divine order is active. If something happens that seems out of sync with that order, I trust God to bring about a solution.

**Divine order is the result of God's spirit at work
in my life and in the world.**

Day 132

— ◆ —

Prayer is a sacred process that gently takes us by the hand and leads us into a greater awareness of the presence of God.—Colleen Zuck

IN GOD'S CARE

Wherever I am, God's spirit is within me and surrounds me. As I start a new job, move to a new home, or begin a new day, I understand that God's presence is there.

When I recognize God's presence in any situation—whether it be a challenge or an opportunity—I feel the expectation of something wonderful building within me. I am alert and fresh, flexible and productive. And if someone or something does not come up to my expectations, I realize that life is about change, growth, and discovery.

What more could I ever ask than for God to be with me in all that I do and everywhere I go? There is no place, no achievement, nothing material that is of more value to me than knowing I am in God's presence and knowing that God loves me.

In God's presence, I feel unconditional love and absolute caring.

Day 133

—◆—

Beloved,

As you turn to Me in prayer, know that there is nothing you can say or do that will cause Me to stop loving you unconditionally. You are My beloved.

Listen, for I will guide you on your path. I will give you encouragement that will enrich your soul and your life.

There is no right or wrong way to speak to Me about your concerns. Whether you bow your head and whisper a prayer or speak to Me with thoughts, I will hear you.

I will answer your prayers. And if the answer is not what you expected to hear, always know that My desire is for what is best for you, My beloved.

"You shall love the Lord your God
with all your heart, and with all your soul,
and with all your might."
—Deuteronomy 6:5

Day 134

—◆—

Expect trouble as an inevitable part of life, and repeat
to yourself the most comforting words of all:
This, too, shall pass.—Ann Landers

RENEWED CREATION There may be times in my life when I will need an extra measure of comfort and reassurance of God's love in order to cope with the unexpected.

In these times, as in all times, God's strength enfolds and protects me in much the same way a cocoon protects a caterpillar as it transforms into a butterfly. I am enfolded by the presence of pure love, and no person or situation can diminish that love.

When the time is right and when I feel strong enough once again in mind and heart, I will emerge as a renewed creation of divine potential.

Both my comfort and my strength come from God, the one source of the divine love and peace that create my reality.

God is my strength and my comfort.

Day 135

—◆—

*To know God is to know love, to give to God is to
give love, to be like God is to be God's love in action.*
—Pauletta Washington

A MESSAGE OF LOVE

As I listen to the guidance I receive from God, I know that I am a living, loving child of divine substance. I am blessed with a wisdom and power that is greater than any power on Earth or in the universe. God created me and gave me life, which is both a precious gift and a tremendous responsibility.

God's message of love for me is an assurance that I will be blessed throughout all eternity. I am cared for, and new avenues of opportunity and fulfillment await me.

God has faith in me to act in responsible ways and to treat others with love and kindness. And for this unconditional love, God asks nothing in return—other than that I accept love and share it as it is given to me—unconditionally. I am love, and I am an expression of divine life, now and forever.

God speaks a message of love to me.

Day 136

— ◆ —

Surrender and trust—
that's the quickest way to heal.
—Ann Marie Davis

DISCOVERY

True freedom is a freedom of spirit which comes from God, a freedom of mind and heart which can never be taken away by people or events. No matter where I am at this moment or what the conditions may be, I can be free.

So I claim my freedom now! I know with every fiber of my being that I am free—free from lack, free from pain, free from doubt, free from anything that would hold me back or keep me from experiencing the wonder and beauty of life.

I am a free and thankful person, declaring, "Thank You, thank You, God, for the freedom to pursue the hopes and dreams that You inspire within me. In Your presence, I discover one of the most precious of all gifts—freedom. I am free to live, to love, and to be at peace."

I am free! Praise God, I am free!

Day 137

♦

You can't expect a 10-dollar answer from a 10-cent prayer. You've got to live your prayer with a God-filled life.—Mary-Alice Jafolla

ANSWERING THE CALL No matter what, there is something I can count on to happen—change. I myself, my world, and everyone and everything in the world are in a constant state of change.

And thank God that this is true. I am unfolding my individual life story. I am never stuck at being the same person, for each day is a day of learning and discovery.

I change outgrown attitudes and beliefs and adopt new ones. I move on to new accomplishments, satisfying a yearning to express the spirit of God that is within me.

I am answering a call to be the creation of God I have always been capable of being. As my life unfolds, there is challenge, but I know that the spirit of God within me is greater than any challenge I can ever meet.

**I answer the call to be the creation of God
I am capable of being.**

Day 138

—◆—

If we have a moral obligation in these times,
it is to be joyful in the face of what we know.
—Elizabeth Roberts

RIGHT PLACE — If I am looking for a job or seeking my right place in the whole scheme of life, I use positive thoughts to direct my thinking. I think of ways I can bless not only myself but also others.

Whatever my own skills may be—working with my hands or with information, working indoors or outdoors—a heartfelt desire to bless is a silent but powerful prayer that will open doors to new and exciting opportunities.

If I am already in my right place, doing what I do best, I give thanks for the blessing of a job which I enjoy and which helps me help others. I am grateful for a work through which God blesses me, my co-workers, and anyone we may help throughout the day. In my right place, I am a blessing to others, and I am blessed in return.

I am in the right place to be a blessing
and to receive a blessing.

Day 139

—◆—

I personally have found that one of the most effective ways of prayer is one of nonresistance . . . of knowing that I can find my good.—Mary L. Kupferle

P O W E R
O F
P R A Y E R

My spiritual journey began with a prayer—quiet words born of a need to know more of the presence of God. And this prayer was also the beginning of a spiritually enriched life.

As my journey continued, I included others in my prayers—family members and friends. Then I embraced all of God's creation in prayers of love and appreciation.

I am travelling far on my spiritual path in reaching an awareness of God that supercedes the need for words. I am becoming one with my prayers by living them out in my life. Each action I take and every thought I think is a reflection of love and faith.

And the journey continues. I may not know what tomorrow will bring, but I do know that each moment is a sacred time with God.

My prayer times are sacred times with God.

Day 140

———◆———

Beloved,

Can you see a sacredness all around you? Can you feel My presence supporting you?

As you let Me guide you, you leave fresh footprints where I have already been. Yet My footsteps echo yours as I walk beside you.

I am all around you: I am the sunshine that warms your body, the leaves that adorn the trees, and the flowers that grace the ground as you walk by.

I am all things to you, and yet more than you could ever possibly imagine. The power and wisdom that are Mine are yours to draw upon at any time.

I am all you will ever need, beloved. Walk with Me and know eternity. Commune with Me and know pure love. Have faith in Me and discover serenity.

"Call to me and I will answer you."
—Jeremiah 33:3

Day 141

———◆———

I believe in recovery, and I believe that as a role model
I have the responsibility to let young people know
that you can make a mistake and come back from it.
—Ann Richards

RECOVERY If I am recovering from an addiction, relationship, or job-related challenge, I may feel incredible stress. But, oh, what relief I experience when I allow the spirit of God to sweep over me and lead me on in recovery!

True recovery is a step-by-step process that heals the heart and restores the soul. God helps me through this process as I learn to let go, release what is worrying me, and be aware of God's presence. The life of God is within me—in every atom of my being.

The life of God is around me, too. And when I honor the divine life within me, I am honoring the divinity within every creation on Earth. Recognizing God's presence everywhere aligns me with the divinity in every moment of life—which leads me to a complete recovery.

The spirit of God heals my heart, restores my soul, and leads me on in recovery.

Day 142

—◆—

*I chose to be a partner with God and
to believe that there was literally nothing impossible for
this partnership.—Mary Manin Morrissey*

VITALLY ALIVE! A positive outlook—a spiritual vision of God as the source of life and renewal—is an important part of my daily health routine. It is the perception of my faith-filled soul that blesses my body.

Starting my day by giving thanks that the very life of God fills me with vitality makes an incredible difference in the way I feel all day long. I know there is renewal constantly going on within me, so I cooperate with the healing that is taking place.

Every thought of or word about my healing is a prayer affirming that the spirit of God is renewing me. An awareness of God's presence within builds on itself minute by minute, hour by hour, day by day. Yes, my spiritual vision of life and health is the perception of my faith-filled soul.

The life of God within me is my vitality.

Day 143

——◆——

One of my characters, Mrs. Cleo Threadgoode, began to teach me about God. I saw God through her eyes. The more I wrote, the more each of my characters helped me begin to believe in God.—Fannie Flagg

GREATNESS OF GOD

God, I am eternally grateful that Your presence is a constant in my life. My faith in You infuses my life with meaning so that whatever I do each day is fulfilling.

I have faith in myself because Your love reassures me and Your wisdom guides me. No task is too great or too small for me—not with Your power and wisdom to guide me.

I have faith in others. We are all Your creations and capable of interacting with each other in total peace and harmony.

God, I have faith in You and Your presence within this world and within all the people who inhabit it. Faith is a great motivator for me to live a life of serenity.

Faith is a powerful motivator in my life.

Day 144

—◆—

Insight comes from looking in.
Spirit is what we see, and that's beautiful!
—Brenda Vaccaro

GOOD NEWS! How do I obtain grace? Well, no amount of study will reveal the formula for it. No good deed will help me earn it. There is absolutely nothing I can do to acquire it.

The good news is that grace is a gift. I do not have to do anything to receive grace! Through God's unconditional love for me, I have been given grace—freely and completely! God's love for me is so great that there is nothing I could ever do which would keep divine grace from me!

Truly there is no greater gift than grace, for through grace God gives abundantly more than anyone could ever need to live life fully. So I rejoice in this precious gift and trust God to give me the wisdom I need to accept it and use it wisely. I begin to understand the depth of God's love.

**Through grace I have the faith and wisdom
to live my life freely and completely.**

DAILY WORD FOR WOMEN

Day 145

—◆—

When we are in divine love, we can experience it as
a tangible force in which we live, move, and have
our being. . . . And when we're in love, we do everything
with love.—Mala Powers

ENVISION LOVE

When I think about all the love I have within me, I realize that I have a lot to give—and I begin by giving forgiveness. As I forgive, something incredible happens within me. Love and understanding move through me first to soothe and heal before reaching out to others.

I forgive the ones I love and even the ones I find difficult to love, because I now understand that they were doing the best they thought they could do at the time. I forgive myself also—for mistakes I have made and for anything I have said or done that I regret.

As I forgive, I envision the love of God radiating from within me and all others. No person or situation in the universe can resist the power of divine love, and I use that divine power each time I forgive.

God's love within me radiates from me as forgiveness.

Day 146

—◆—

Like Dad, I want people to believe in God and
to have hope. We are all gifts of God. We are all miracles.
Sometimes we just forget.—Cheryl Landon

HEART-AND-SOUL CONNECTION I have only to think of the people who have made an important contribution in my life to actually feel loved and supported.

I remember those who have always been there for me—family, lifelong friends, and companions. Maybe several outstanding people come to mind: parents, teachers, and mentors who encouraged me along in different stages of life. Or perhaps in one brief moment someone believed in me and helped me have confidence for a lifetime.

Such heart-and-soul connections are spiritual in nature, because they spring from a commitment to God. Out of a commitment to God comes a dedication to love, listen to, and understand others.

My commitment to God blesses me
and all my relationships.

Day 147

—◆—

Beloved,

Whatever you are going through, I will help you. I am here for you whether you think you need Me or not. You will never need to go through anything alone, for I will be here, encouraging you every moment of the day or night.

I am the strength you need to overcome any obstacle in your way. I am the courage you need to face life with confidence. I am the very life within you, life that is eternal and whole.

Allow yourself to feel My love for you and within you. Accept My love, and use it to help yourself and others. In everything you do, rely on Me and trust in Me. My spirit within you is ready to express love and understanding, life and courage through you and as you.

You are My beloved, and I am right here with you—now and forever.

"I will comfort you."
—Isaiah 66:13

Day 148

—◆—

*God has given us so much that we are unable
to know it all. It is God's very nature to give
and give and give.—Mary-Alice Jafolla*

**GIVER
OF LIFE**
God, there is nothing in life that I
receive more fulfillment, joy, and
satisfaction from than being totally
aware of You.

You are the creator, sustainer, and eternal spirit of life.
As I think of what truly nourishes me in spirit, mind,
and body, I understand that You are the source of all
blessings.

God, I pray not from a sense of need but from a
desire to know always that You are with me. You are
the giver of life—the constant source of all that enables
me to express and experience life.

You have shown me that the true way of life is to live
in the awareness of Your presence. I have a powerful
sense of You, God—of Your spirit within me, within
others, and within every experience.

**God is my creator and the source of all
that prospers me.**

Day 149

—◆—

God is this eternal life
that we make into living.
—*Myrtle Fillmore*

GOD IS
WITH ME
For the most part, a vacation or even a change of scenery can be such a freeing experience. Yet I know that I am the same person whether I am at home or in a hotel room far from home, in a huge city or in a remote countryside.

So what is it that gives me that feeling of freedom when I travel to new or more relaxing surroundings? I have left behind the excess baggage of worry or concern and made sure I have taken my faith in God with me.

The truth of the matter is that if I take worry or concern with me on a trip or vacation, I will not—cannot—be free to enjoy myself and my new surroundings, to relax with my family and friends.

Yes, freedom is something I can have no matter where I am, because no matter where I am, God is with me.

Wherever I am, I am free,
for I have freedom of spirit.

Day 150

—◆—

Great opportunities to help others seldom come,
but small ones surround us every day.
—Sally Koch

SPIRIT OF GIVING The Golden Rule reminds me to treat others as I want to be treated. And I can live the Golden Rule by giving my family, friends, and community the same kind of love, understanding, and appreciation I want to receive from them.

I give love and kindness to my family and friends, which reassures them that they can turn to me for support and understanding in any situation. I am filled with the spirit of giving.

I give my time and creativity to the community around me. Wherever I am needed, I am there to offer an encouraging word or a helping hand.

The presence of God is within me and is being expressed through me in a spirit of giving.

I am a loving, giving spiritual being.

A SECOND CHANCE

BY SISTER MARY ROSE CHRISTY

When Ionica was found in a desolate area of woods, he appeared to be about three years old. The story told was that he had been raised by wolves. Unable to talk, he communicated with sounds—growls and barks—much the way a pup would. Some loose hair on his body was examined and determined to be from wolves.

We will never know for sure if Ionica was really raised by wolves, but we do know that he was born in Romania during a time of great hardship. The economy was poor. In order to build a large workforce, the president issued an edict that any woman with fewer than five children would be heavily taxed. Many parents struggling to feed large families abandoned their children, believing they would be better off in an orphanage.

Soon after Ionica was found, he was brought to Riul Vadului, an orphanage in a remote area of Transylvania. Given a second chance in life, he has flourished. He speaks well and has become the peacemaker at the orphanage. Hidden deep within his mind is the story of his first three years of life, but—thank God—that unusual start has left not a trace of an imprint on the tall, handsome man of today.

Day 151

—◆—

Since we live and move and have our being in God,
whatever we are saying or doing, we are saying
and doing in the presence of God, and every word
or act is a kind of prayer.—Hypatia Hasbrouck

SPIRITUAL AWARENESS Today is a celebration like no other, for it is a holy rejoicing. So I begin by taking a moment to become quiet, to take my attention within to the source of my life and love and intelligence.

In this supreme moment of awareness, I feel totally connected to God in mind, body, and spirit. I discover the truth of my being: I can never be separated from the presence of God.

This is a celebration of spiritual awareness; I am eternally alive with the life of God! From this moment on, I will consciously live my life in an awareness of the spirit of God within me.

The breath of the Almighty has given me life, and each breath I take is a celebration of divine life.

I celebrate life!

Day 152

—◆—

Anyone who holds firmly to faith
in divine order can prove the power of God.
—Martha Smock

GOD SPEAKS TO ME

God speaks to me in gentle ways. When the wind touches my face, I am reminded of God's presence in my life. And it is the gentle, yet powerful, presence of Spirit that brings order to my life.

Everyone and everything created is a reflection of God's order. I am thankful for the perfect way my body was designed to work—how it efficiently processes the nutrients I take in and then transforms those nutrients into energy that I can use.

I am grateful for the way events unfold in an orderly way. Even when I am not aware of the order in some experience, I know that order is there because God is there.

God is everywhere, shining forth from the people I meet, the decisions I make, and everything I do.

My life is in divine order because God, and the order of God, is everywhere.

Day 153

—◆—

*There is no reason for us to lose
the feeling of limitless energy.*
—Connie Fillmore Bazzy

INSPIRATION OF SPIRIT

I know the benefits of eating fresh fruits and vegetables: They are brimming with vitamins and nutrition! Yet if left on the shelf, they will spoil and will need to be discarded.

Understanding the benefits of freshness, I never let stale, negative thoughts or ideas linger in my mind. I release them and then turn to Spirit within for a fresh supply of wisdom. I am totally alive—mind, body, and soul—through the power of Spirit Divine!

I am refreshed each day as I allow my thoughts to be inspired by God. Then my mind is focused, and I am ready to recognize every golden opportunity.

I am a powerhouse of divine energy and vitality! I direct that momentum toward accomplishing whatever it is that I am to do and experience each day.

I am refreshed by the inspiration of Spirit!

Day 154

— ◆ —

Beloved,

I am the life within every cell of your body, so you have the strength and stamina you need for this and every day.

No matter what responsibilities are yours to fulfill, know that I am guiding you and inspiring you every step of the way.

Live each moment in the spirit of love—which is My spirit within you. Let Me speak to you and through you as love and compassion. I am the love and joy that will heal and transform you.

Hour by hour, minute by minute, you are becoming more aware that it is My spirit within you which sets you free!

"The spirit of God has made me, and the breath of the Almighty gives me life."
—Job 33:4

Day 155

———◆———

Happiness—pure joy—is from within.
It is a spiritual entity, a free . . . gift of God.
—Dana Gatlin

LIGHTNESS OF BEING The greatest joy in my life is more than a cheerful emotion. It is a state of being, of knowing I am spiritually alive!

Of course I feel happy and lighthearted when I am with the people I love. However, there is a pure joy of spirit that I experience when I make a divine connection with God.

I feel such gratitude rising within me when I understand that God cares for me and about me. This understanding encourages me to experience the joy of spirit at all times.

Even when outer conditions might not seem promising, I am filled with a "lightness of being." Pure joy does not necessarily mean that I am laughing and joking—it is the exhilaration of truly knowing I am alive and one with God.

I am filled with a "lightness of being,"
of being spiritually alive!

Day 156

—◆—

Think of God as
the very Spirit within you.
—May Rowland

GOD CARES FOR ME

When I pray, I understand that it is God, not me, who knows best. God is constantly loving me and caring for me, and it is my responsibility to cooperate with God—not outline what I think should happen.

So I release all concern and pray. I remove my own ego from the situation and allow the will of God to be fully realized in me and through me. As I release feelings of uncertainty, I feel the powerful presence of God enfold me.

I give thanks for the divine order that is governing every situation in my life and the lives of all I hold dear. I trust God because I know that each time I do, I am opening the door to endless possibilities.

God cares for me and works wonders through me.

I am blessed by God's presence and care.

Day 157

$-\blacklozenge-$

When we are filled with joy, we are at one with
the universe, and the harmony . . . of God fills us.
—Mary L. Kupferle

DIVINE
SHIFT

Turning hostility into hospitality or resentment into acceptance is a matter of choice. And these are my choices so that I can live in spiritual harmony with others.

So instead of thinking about what may be wrong with others and in my relationships with them, I focus on what seems right. Something powerful emerges from this observation: Little annoyances fade away, and a reverence for the sacredness of all people increases.

When I am willing to accept all others as God's creations of life and love, a shift occurs in me. And often, the change in my own attitude draws a like response from others.

An expression of acceptance can be all that is needed to bridge any gap of misunderstanding. Love will then forge a connection of harmony and goodwill.

I live in spiritual harmony with others.

Day 158

— ◆ —

*Our objective is to learn how to use the power
of thought in such a way that it will help to make our
dreams come true.—Stella Terrill Mann*

**REST
IN THE
PRESENCE**
When I allow myself to do nothing
but rest in the presence of God, I think
thoughts that bless me. I relax and
know that giving my time to God is
the greatest investment I can make.

When I give my attention to God, I am preparing
myself for whatever is ahead. Whenever change occurs,
I understand that it is a turning point which leads me to
new opportunities, such as moving up or moving on in
my career, forming new friendships or renewing ones
that are already established.

What is most important for me to remember is that
each quiet moment with God is an opportunity for
spiritual renewal.

**Today is a turning point which leads
to new opportunities.**

Day 159

———◆———

At the great heart of humanity there is a deep ... home-sickness that never has been and never can be satisfied with anything less than a clear, vivid consciousness of the indwelling presence of God.—H. Emilie Cady

ALWAYS HOME

Whether I am returning home from a business trip or vacation, I feel relief and contentment stir within me when I see the first familiar landmark. Yet no matter how far I may travel from my family, friends, or community, I am always at home with God.

The spirit of God is within me wherever I may go. Knowing this, I experience an inner peace which nourishes my soul. I have spiritual strength that empowers me to face any situation with calm resolve.

As I bask in the warm glow of God's peace, I hear the gentle whisper of inspiration in my heart: "Rest, for you are safe with Me. Be at peace, for I am with you."

God assures me that I am not alone.

Day 160

— ◆ —

Our good is nothing less than the realization
of complete oneness with God.
—Elizabeth Sand Turner

WELCOME! God created each and every person, and the spirit of God lives within all people.

From God's spirit within me, I reach out to others with understanding and acceptance. Each person I meet is so very important, and my welcome to them is from one member of God's family to another!

It doesn't matter what differences may exist between us, for it is our shared spirituality that brings us together. As we help and support each other, we are letting the spirit of God weave us together in love.

So I welcome others into my heart. I welcome them into my prayers. I welcome them into a circle of love. As I join with others in thought and prayer, I am also joining with them in making a commitment to fill the world with an awareness of God and divine love.

I am a welcome member of God's universal family!

Day 161

---◆---

Beloved,

I welcome the times we spend together, for you are My precious child.

You are growing and unfolding every day into a more magnificent creation. You are filled with unlimited potential as you let My presence be expressed in and through everything you do.

My blessings are always with you, and I love you. So let go of worry, let go of fear, let go of any anxiety that might hold you back. Keep your mind and your heart focused on what you know is right for you, and I will take care of the rest.

When you are finished with what is yours to do this day, come home to Me. I will give you the rest you need to feel refreshed and ready to begin again.

"I have said these things to you
so that my joy may be in you,
and that your joy may be complete."
—John 15:11

Day 162

—◆—

Men judge us by the success of our efforts.
God looks at the efforts themselves.
—Charlotte Brontë

LOVING HEART
Each day, I bless all those whose jobs include caring for the well-being of others. I know that they are being blessed as they bless others.

I also remember that the role of caregiver is not limited to those who care for people. So I extend blessings to those who take care of pets and wildlife as well. The nurturing of all forms of life requires a loving heart, patience, and kindness.

Also included in my prayers are those who are dedicated to caring for a loved one or friend. Whether it is a son or daughter caring for an elderly parent or a neighbor helping the person next door, they are all generous people. They are acting from God's love within, and they are important role models for us all.

Thank You, God, for blessing my life
with caring individuals.

Day 163

—◆—

A whisper can be stronger, as an atom
is stronger, than a whole mountain.
—Louise Nevelson

GENTLE There is incredible power in gentleness. A gentle touch can reduce another person's emotional stress and ease their physical pain. A kind word spoken from the heart can melt any resistance to harmony and mutual understanding between people.

Gentleness is an innate quality of spirit that enriches my life and strengthens my character. It is compassion born of my spiritual nature that prompts the decisions I make and the actions I take.

The tenderness I give to those who need someone to lean on for support or direction is my own inner peace radiating out from me in times of love and compassion.

I am a gentle and kind creation of my loving Creator.

Day 164

———◆———

For the truly faithful,
no miracle is necessary.
—Nancy Gibbs

I AM READY

Through my faith, I know beyond any doubt that God created me to be happy. So how could I ever doubt that God created me with all I need to live my life to the fullest? I do not, for I do not doubt God!

I give thanks for the blessings I already have and get ready for the new blessings God has in store for me! I am thankful for my life and for the lives of the ones I hold dear. It is God's life within that connects us in love.

I give thanks for the beauty I see all around me and for the beauty that is within each and every child of God. God's spirit is within all people, so I recognize that each and every person is a wonder to behold.

Most of all, I am thankful for God's love within me. Through divine love, I am aware of the blessings I have and am prepared for the blessings that are on their way to me.

I am ready for the blessings God has for me.

Day 165

———— ◆ ————

We forget all too soon the things
we thought we could never forget.
—Joan Didion

FOREVER YOUNG

There is a familiar adage that says "You're only as old as you feel," and isn't this the truth? No matter how mature I am in human terms, I am forever young in spirit because I have God's eternal spirit of life, love, and joy within.

And it is the life of God within me that acts as a spiritual battery continually recharging me and giving me the strength to carry on. When I feel God's love within me, I am tapping into the true fountain of life—a fountain that can never run dry.

I feel joy within! It is this joy that energizes me and gives me the desire to try new things, to continue to learn and grow and discover more of God in my life.

I am forever one with God, forever young in spirit, forever one with the source of true happiness and peace.

I am forever young in spirit.

Day 166

—◆—

Life's challenges are not supposed to paralyze you,
they're supposed to help you discover who you are.
—*Bernice Johnson Reagon*

STEADY ASSURANCE I never want to overlook a solution because I am so caught up in the problem. So I make it a point to allow my belief in the power and the presence of God to be my focus.

I believe in God, and that belief supports me during any challenge and inspires me to succeed. As I trust God to guide me, I create an atmosphere around me that nurtures me.

God is both the giver and sustainer of my life, and I know that God is constantly pouring out pure, unconditional love to me. Whenever I take my awareness away from the confusion around me, the assurance of God satisfies the longing of my soul.

God's steady assurance tells me that I will never have to face anything alone. God is my life and my constant companion.

God, I believe in the wonder of Your power
and presence.

Day 167

—◆—

*I believe strongly in the gospel that says you help
people who are hungry and you help people
who are suffering, and you help people who need help.*
—*Marian Wright Edelman*

SHINING EXAMPLE Every time I pray, I remember to bless my loved ones in my prayers. I do this because I love them and want what is best for them. We may have had differences in the past, but that doesn't change the fact that I love and appreciate each one. Their presence in my life is a blessing I will always cherish.

My joy in being with friends and family is a reflection of divine joy within me. I pray that my gladness prompts them to remember their own inner joy and continue to express it.

In everything my loved ones do, I see them expressing God's life and love. As they recognize these qualities within themselves, they can't help but be shining examples to others, helping them to know that we are all eternally one with God and one with each other.

I bless my loved ones in my prayers.

Day 168

—◆—

Beloved,

You are precious to me in this moment and in every moment that has been or will ever be! Even in your times of greatest challenge, your indomitable strength and courage will prevail, for I am your strength of mind, body, and spirit.

Whenever you need to talk, I will listen. Whenever you need rest, I will give you peace of mind and body. When you need comfort, you can count on Me to give you all the help that is Mine to give.

I am the wisdom that surpasses all the ages, and I am the understanding that created and continues to guide the world. I will always have time for you, I will always love you, and I will always uphold you.

> *"When you call upon me . . .*
> *I will hear you."*
> *—Jeremiah 29:12*

Day 169

Genius is the gold in the mine; talent
is the miner who works and brings it out.
—Marguerite Blessington

LIGHT IN THE WORLD

There is a light in the world that outshines any light made by human hands and radiates with an energy far greater than the sun. This tremendous light is the presence of God.

A spark of faith within me draws my attention to God as the spirit of divine life and wisdom within my soul. And just as oxygen is necessary in keeping a fire burning, my awareness is essential in keeping me always turned toward the light of God within me.

The light of God within me shines brighter and brighter until I am aglow with divine energy. I am one with the eternal light of God. The darkness of doubt is gone forever, for a spark of faith has filled me with the light of God.

**I am a light of divine energy that radiates
out into the world.**

Day 170

—◆—

Each one of us has a fire in our heart for something.
It's our goal in life to find it and to keep it lit.
—Mary Lou Retton

AUTHENTIC When I have tried to live up to the dreams and expectations of someone else, I soon discovered that those dreams and expectations could never make me happy.

I realize it is only through following my own inner guidance, through letting God inspire me, that I can be happy with who I am.

God's loving spirit is always with me to guide me in being the unique person I am meant to be. And when I am being that person, I have so much to give to the world! I have so much within me which is mine alone to give.

So I live in celebration of my authenticity! By being true to myself, I discover what it really means to be God's creation of life.

As I give what is mine to give, I am being
the authentic me that God created.

Day 171

—◆—

Your body cannot heal without play.
Your mind cannot heal without laughter.
Your soul cannot heal without joy.
—Catherine Rippenger Fenwick

VISUALIZE HEALING God has given me a body that is spontaneously able to heal itself. So I cooperate with my body's own natural healing ability by praying for and keeping positive thoughts about it. Healing accelerates in the sacred environment of prayer.

And if I am going through some kind of treatment—from vitamins to medication—I allow whatever I take into my body to do its best work when I cooperate with it and do not resist it.

So I visualize the treatment as something that is helping me—a strengthening, healing energy that is moving throughout my body and restoring me. I see—ahead of the actual results—the wholeness that I am becoming more and more each day.

I use spiritual vision to cooperate with the healing that is taking place now.

Day 172

—◆—

*When you are kind to someone in trouble, you hope
they'll remember and be kind to someone else.
And it'll become like a wildfire.*—*Whoopi Goldberg*

**GOD'S
SKILLFUL
MASTERY**
Each key on a piano plays a single note. But in the skillful hands of a pianist, these individual keys work in harmony with each other to create beautiful music.

Similarly, I am an individual with my own notes to sound. With God as the master musician, I blend with others in beautiful harmony. Infused with love and understanding, compassion and forgiveness, I work with others to create beautiful chords of harmony.

In tune with God's love, I am fulfilling my destiny of spiritual oneness. And I am helping create a peaceful, love-filled world for all those who will follow in my footsteps.

I am in harmony with God's peace and love.

Day 173

—◆—

A clay pot sitting in the sun will always be a clay pot.
It has to go through the white heat of the furnace
to become porcelain.—Mildred Witte Stouven

SACRED INTER-MISSION Sometimes it seems that just when I am finally making progress toward some goal or project, everything suddenly comes to a standstill.

Maybe this seemingly negative happening is, in fact, a positive one, an intermission that allows me to consider other options, enjoy a needed break, or improve on my plans. Perhaps this intermission is essential to my spiritual growth—a time of moving my attention away from the busyness around me to the quiet of my own inner refuge of peace.

There I experience a sacred reunion with the presence of God. Lingering in the presence of God, I realize what it feels like to be at peace.

In the quiet haven of my soul, I meet with the presence of God.

Day 174

—◆—

It is not of so much consequence what you say,
as how you say it.
—Alexandra Smith

GOD'S LOVING TOUCH

Closer than the air I breathe, God is with me. And whenever I seek reassurance or comfort, I know that God is there to listen.

"Hello, God. It's me, and I need You. My heart is yearning for You, for only You can give me the peace I desire. I know You will help me, God, by filling me with Your love. Through Your loving touch I experience the peace that will help me carry on.

"Today, I need strength for myself and also added strength to help others. When my own human efforts are not enough, Your love and peace will lift me above my own limitations to a place where I cannot fail.

"I believe in You, God, and I need Your help right now, so that I can also believe in myself and in the endless possibilities for me. Right here—enfolded in Your love, sustained by Your strength, and soothed by Your peace—I do believe."

The peace of God soothes me.

Day 175

—◆—

Beloved,

Filled with life and strength, you are capable of living your dreams to the full satisfaction of your soul.

You are growing and thriving in every moment of life, for within your physical body is a spiritual source of life and vitality that is continually healing and renewing you.

Know that you are never without the support and love and acceptance you desire. I am with you, supplying you with strength and wisdom and comfort—confirmation of My love for you.

In the quietness of your soul, I speak to you. With your heart and mind, listen to what I say. Trust in Me. Love Me. Let Me guide you in all that you do. You are My beloved, and I care about you.

*"This is my prayer, that your love
may overflow more and more
with knowledge and full insight to help
you to determine what is best."
—Philippians 1:9–10*

Day 176

—◆—

With the eye on faith,
you see God in all.
—Martha Smock

FAITH

Faith serves as a ladder—a tool I use to rise above any challenge. With faith, I am able to get through whatever happens in my life because I understand that I am a part of the divine design of the universe in which I live. I realize that challenges are chances for growth.

My faith in God just naturally leads me to giving thanks to God. Thanksgiving is one of the greatest gifts I can give—not only to God but to myself and my loved ones as well. Just being in an atmosphere of thanksgiving enriches me and those around me.

God's wisdom and power are supreme. I feel such assurance knowing that as I turn to God in making any decision, I will be guided. I have faith in God, the creator of the universe and my own personal guide.

I have absolute faith in God, whose wisdom
and power are supreme.

Day 177

---◆---

Right now we are in the creative process
of bringing forth a world from the living Spirit
that dwells within.—Sue Sikking

SWEET SPIRIT

Sweet Spirit of life, shine Your light on me and show me the way. I am placing my trust in You, knowing that You will never fail me. Guide me and help me to know what I need to know.

Fill me with Your peace, and give me the strength to carry on. In this and every moment, give me the courage to do what I must to follow Your will.

I feel Your love, sweet Spirit, and I am grateful for Your understanding and compassion. But above all else, I am grateful for Your wisdom and light and unfailing direction.

Although there may be times when I feel uncertain, I know this is okay. I also know that Your shining light will dispel the darkness of human fears and help me overcome every challenge life may bring. Thank You, thank You, sweet Spirit of life!

Thank You, thank You, sweet Spirit of life,
for shining Your light on me.

Day 178

—◆—

In the silence we get the wonderful
inward joy that is of God.
—Myrtle Fillmore

GREATEST JOY Joy is so much more than just a feeling of happiness and lightheartedness. And I am thankful that I realize my greatest joy emanates from knowing God.

I know the joy of spirit! And such joy translates into a contentment and satisfaction I feel in knowing who I am: a spiritual being going through the human experience.

I know the joy of loving, for it is divine love that created me to love and be loved. I appreciate family and friends. God loves me and has placed these people here with me to share my life and to bless me with their love and understanding.

I know the joy of oneness with God, a joy that empowers me to be the greatest blessing I can be. There is a continual flow of divine energy that courses throughout my mind and body. I know and feel the joy of spirit.

My greatest joy is knowing and expressing
the joy of spirit!

Day 179

—◆—

*Everyone has a gift for something,
even if it is the gift of being a good friend.*
—Marian Anderson

**BEING A
BLESSING**
Here I am, God. My heart and mind
are open, and I am ready to do
whatever I can to be a blessing.

Speak through me, God, so that my
voice will give comfort and assurance to others. Teach
me to choose and use the words and actions that will
help others the most and reassure them in their times of
greatest need.

I want to inspire others to know You better. So guide
my steps and lead me to the people who need support,
encouragement, and love.

I am ready, God, to be a blessing. Move through me
to bless others so that they may overcome doubt and
fear—anything which might make them feel separate
from You. I feel Your love, God, and I am eager for each
opportunity to share Your love with others.

Here I am, God, ready to be a blessing.

Day 180

◆

My favorite thing is to go
where I've never been.
—Diane Arbus

STARTING OVER At times, the last word I want to hear is change. And rightly so, for I may feel comfortable in my job, with my family, and in my home. Then, one day, a change occurs and a move or a separation seems to turn my world upside down!

I can turn my world right side up by viewing the change in my own mind as something that will be a positive rather than a negative.

This positive way of looking at change broadens my outlook so that I understand there are choices I can make, new adventures I will enjoy, and talents and skills I will reveal. I appreciate that, in a world of God's creation, every day can be a chance to start over and be more loving, understanding, and prosperous.

Thank You, God, for a new start—a day
in which I can be more and do more.

THE BRIGHTER OUTCOME

BY JAYNE MEADOWS

Pain in my stomach—so severe it doubled me over—sent me to the hospital. My doctor examined me and discovered a very large growth that hadn't been there just a month before when I had my yearly checkup. He explained, "I want you to go home now, pack your suitcase, and come back to the hospital in the morning. And Jayne, be prepared for an operation. This could be a fast-growing cancer."

Early the next morning, I was about to go out the door with my suitcase in hand when I thought of Silent Unity. Through years of reading *Daily Word*, I knew about the Silent Unity prayer ministry, but I had never called with a prayer request.

Now I knew I must call! I never go anywhere without my *Daily Word*, so I retrieved the current issue from my suitcase, found the telephone number, and called. A person with a gentle, soothing voice answered and prayed a beautiful, heartfelt prayer. I felt so much better, so at peace.

I had all kinds of tests at the hospital. The next day, my doctor said, "Jayne, we're going to operate tomorrow—exploratory surgery." He explained the whole procedure and then advised me to be sure to get a good night's sleep.

But I couldn't sleep, so I began to record messages for my husband, Steve, and my son, Bill, on the cassette recorder I had brought with me. I did this so that no matter what happened to me, my son could hear his mother's voice telling him how much she loves him and what a great young man he is. I recorded many different messages—one for his next birthday, one for next Christmas, one he could hear on Easter, even one for his graduation! He was only nine years old, yet I felt as if suddenly I had to tell him all the things a mother would say over the whole lifetime of her child.

Just as I finished recording, two young interns came into my room. They started to ask me questions the other doctors had never asked me. One intern said, "When do you remember first getting this pain?"

"Oh, the first time I had it was a good 15 or 20 years ago. I've had it every once in a while, but I was always able to cure it myself. It was much worse this time."

At that moment, the doctor who was to do my surgery entered the room with his right arm in a sling! I thought, "He's going to operate on me?"

One of the interns said, "Doctor, we would like to talk to you about this case. We think you should call off the exploratory surgery and let us do one more test. This could be diverticulitis."

"How do you like these punks telling me what to do?" he asked.

"Well, with what I'm facing, doctor, I think you should listen to these punks," I said, "and call off the operation for at least one more day."

The doctor seemed convinced, saying, "All right, we'll call it off."

I stayed in the hospital another week, on a strict diet and with bed rest. I was released at the end of the week with the understanding that I would be an outpatient for six months. During that time, the extreme case of diverticulitis began to heal. I've had to follow a specific diet from that day to this, but I did not have to have surgery.

I believe that my call to Silent Unity's prayer room gave me the peace I needed to think clearly and not just go along with having surgery that was not needed. I had hope, so I didn't give over the control of my life, not even to my doctor. I also believe prayer drew those wonderful interns to my aid. They helped hand my life back to me.

And it's been a wonderful life—one in which I've been able to watch my son grow up, marry, have children, and become a successful television producer.

When the first diagnosis of cancer was given to me, I did do some preparing for the worst, but I'm a very optimistic person. I prayed and believed that there would be a much brighter outcome. Thank God, my prayers were answered.

Day 181

$\blacklozenge$

*Boundless energy and enthusiasm for life are inherent
in each of us, as evidenced by the nature of the child.*
—Connie Fillmore Bazzy

ENTHUSIASM Something is rising within me and shining out from me. It is my enthusiasm for life! I am alive with the life of God, and I am excited about all the possibilities that are before me!

Never before and never again will I have the exact opportunities that today will bring, so I look forward to each moment of the day as a new adventure—a new adventure in living, a new adventure in loving, a new adventure in proving to myself that I have potential.

I am energized! I am free! I am eager to participate in life! I am filled with an enthusiasm that affects everything I do—from routine tasks to projects which require special attention. In fact, everything I do is cast in the glow of my positive, enthusiastic attitude.

I am enthusiastic about life!

Day 182

———◆———

Beloved,

Relax and listen as I tell you how thankful I am for you.

Each time you let the anger or upset of others be filtered through your nonresistant attitude, you give a blessing. Your soft, gentle answers reach out as love and understanding to calm others and to soothe their pain.

Your joy in giving expression to My spirit within you is something magnificent to behold. The encouragement you give to others blesses them—and you, as well, because every blessing you release into the world returns to you enhanced and multiplied.

You handle change with an enthusiasm that lights up the very atmosphere around you. I give thanks, beloved, that you bring harmony to your relationships and circumstances.

"May the Lord direct your hearts
to the love of God and
to the steadfastness of Christ."
—2 Thessalonians 3:5

Day 183

—◆—

I think self-awareness is probably the most important
thing toward being a champion.
—Billie Jean King

**THE
WONDER
OF ME**

If ever I doubt that I am a divine creation, I take a moment to look at the wonder which is my body.

I consider my hands: Beneath the skin lies an intricate network of delicate bones and muscles that work in harmony with my brain. I think of all the signals which must be sent out and the responses which must happen in order for me to pick up a coin or dial a telephone!

My heart and lungs work 24 hours a day to supply the blood and oxygen I need. My brain also works nonstop—controlling both physical and mental tasks—and all with little or no conscious effort from me.

The attention to detail that God gave to life is evident in me. So as I consider the wonders my body performs every day, I can't help but thank God for the wonder of me!

God, I thank You for the wonder of me!

Day 184

—◆—

Faith is the first factor in a life devoted to service.
Without it, nothing is possible. With it, nothing
is impossible.—Mary McLeod Bethune

REASSURANCE When I am in the position of making a decision—whether at work or in my personal life—I want and need reassurance that what I am doing is the right thing.

I don't take the responsibility of decision making lightly, especially when my decisions impact the lives of others. I trust my judgment and know that divine order is governing not only our lives, but also the lives of all humankind and the entire universe.

God's love is strong enough to still raging waters, yet gentle enough to soothe the tender soul. When I turn to God for reassurance, I am inspired with peace and understanding.

My decisions are born of wisdom and acted upon with the strength of spirit that can only come from God.

God is my source of understanding
and constant reassurance.

Day 185

❖

*A smile is a curve
that sets everything straight.*
—Phyllis Diller

SMILE

Perhaps there is no other sign in the world that conveys friendship, love, and peace in a more universally understood way than a smile. A smile is a message of acceptance and gladness from one person to another.

So I choose to smile and let my smiles make an unmistakable statement about me: I'm accepting and friendly. And the response I receive is fantastic—friends and strangers, adults and children, my pets and the pets of others know from a simple facial expression the gladness that fills me.

A smile is a happy, uplifting thought that I release to shine out into the atmosphere around me. It is as though I am opening the window of my soul in order to experience the love of God that lives within me and to share that experience with others.

**Each smile I give is a powerful message
of friendship and love.**

Day 186

—◆—

*I have always grown from my problems
and challenges, from the things that don't work out;
that's when I've really learned.—Carol Burnett*

**EVERLASTING
COMFORT**

As a child, I may have felt great comfort when snuggling with a favorite blanket or being hugged by my parents or grandparents. And while the blanket and the hugs offered comfort, it was temporary and lasted only until the next challenge to my confidence or feelings of security.

Now I understand that everlasting comfort comes from knowing God's presence in my life. In prayers of thanksgiving, I enfold myself in God's comfort and peace:

"O loving Spirit, You are the air which I breathe, the earth which I walk on, the love which I feel in my heart. Thank You, thank You, God, for life. Thank You for being my comfort in every moment of life."

I live in the assurance of everlasting comfort from God.

Day 187

—◆—

The healthy, the strong individual is the one
who asks for help when he needs it.
—Rona Barrett

G O D
H E A L S
A L L

God's healing life flows through me, renewing my mind and healing my body. I am vitally alive!

God is with me to give me all the strength, all the energy, all the help I could ever possibly need. And believing that total health is possible for me is important, for the simple act of allowing my body to relax opens it up to a continual flow of God's healing life. As I place my trust in God, I am allowing a divine, restorative work to go on within me.

And if, at any time, I begin to tense up or feel overwhelmed by all that is going on in and around me, I remember that God heals all of me—my mind, my body, and my emotions.

I am healed through and through, for it is the spirit of the Almighty that heals me.

God's spirit within heals me.

Day 188

—◆—

You may be disappointed if you fail,
but you are doomed if you don't try.
—Beverly Sills

SPIRITUAL JOURNEY Some of the greatest inventions came about only after years of failed experiments. For scientists and inventors, those failed attempts were learning experiences that helped them in their discoveries.

Seeming failures can be learning experiences for me, too. When I am in search of my own discoveries, I remember that failures can bring me closer to success; they are a process of elimination in which each one brings me closer to the perfect solution.

On my spiritual journey, I am continually making discoveries about myself—who I am and what I am capable of through the power of God within.

If I have made errors in judgment or blunders in past actions, I see them as learning experiences and build upon them. I, too, am on my way to great discoveries.

I am moving forward on a spiritual journey
of great discovery.

Day 189

———◆———

Beloved,

Celebrate all that you are, all that you are becoming! The radiant beauty of your smile is a reflection of the light that is glowing within you. Let your light shine for all to see and know that you are a source of both comfort and joy for others.

Your life is a magnificent journey—a spiritual journey in which you will discover what you are capable of achieving. Always be the best you can be, do the best you are capable of doing. When you do, you truly will be celebrating life.

Do not be afraid, for I am with you all the way. Let My love be a healing balm that gently soothes you. Rest assured that with every step you take, you are walking a path that will lead you to greater and greater accomplishments.

"The darkness is passing away
and the true light is already shining."
—1 John 2:8

Day 190

—◆—

My personal hobbies are reading,
listening to music, and silence.
—Edith Sitwell

REST AND RELAX   In the presence of God, I become quiet and invite divine peace to fill every cell of my body. As I rest in silence, I am aware only of the holy presence. A wave of calm moves through me and I rest.

In the presence of God, I relax and open my mind to divine wisdom. With an open mind and heart, I am more receptive to the blessings that are mine to claim.

In the presence of God, I take a break from the pressures around me and release all concerns. I simply rest and relax. As I breathe in and out, I acknowledge God as the one and only power in my life, as the source of all I could ever need or desire.

In the presence of God, there is nothing in the world which can disturb the calm peace of my soul.

In the presence of God, I rest and relax.

Day 191

——◆——

For every failure, there's an alternative course of action.
You just have to find it. When you come to a roadblock,
take a detour.—Mary Kaye Ashe

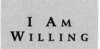

**I Am
Willing**

God, I know with my whole being
that if there is anything I need to be
free from, You are willing to let it
happen. You are willing to uphold me
in expressing my creative best.

Now I say to You, "Yes, God, I am willing." And
when my will is a reflection of Your will, I am free. I am
free from any habit or tendency that might limit me. I
am free to explore my heart's desire and also to
accomplish it.

I have faith in You, God, and I am willing to let my
faith be renewed every moment of every day. I realize
that some days will be more challenging than others.
But whatever willingness I am able to express will be
multiplied and returned to me as an awareness of my
spiritual freedom.

Yes, God, I am willing.

**I am willing to live my life as the spiritually free child
of God that I truly am.**

Day 192

—◆—

Never fear shadows. They simply mean there's
a light shining somewhere nearby.
—Ruth E. Renkel

DIVINE MESSAGE I can learn so much about myself when I truly listen to myself—to my own thoughts and my conversations with others.

Yet there is a deeper level of listening that brings out an even greater understanding. In silence, I listen to the indwelling spirit of God. The message I listen to is one of grace: God's assurance that I am loved unconditionally.

And the wonder of grace is this: The more I listen to its message of love and acceptance, the more I want to be loving and accepting of myself and others. Grace— God's love in action—builds me up and directs me in living a life that blesses me and others.

Thank You, God, for Your message of unconditional love.

Day 193

—◆—

Life is a succession of moments.
To live each one is to succeed.
—Corita Kent

GOLDEN MOMENTS Sometimes I wish I had it all—all I think I need or should have. Yet when I clear away the confusion over wants and needs, I understand that it is the simple things in life—the golden times—that mean the most to me.

Golden moments are filled with the people and experiences that bring me the greatest fulfillment. They may be times of togetherness with family and friends, enjoying conversation and laughter. Or they may be times away from everyone as I simply relax in blessed solitude for a few moments.

I realize that any success or prosperity I have enjoyed is most accurately measured by what has touched my heart and warmed my soul. And the most golden of moments can happen again and again—every time I realize that God's spirit lives within me.

Each moment that I am aware of You, God,
is a golden moment in my life.

Day 194

—◆—

Forgiveness does not deny anger
but faces it head-on.
—Alice Miller

BEYOND APPEARANCES   I may hear of or see people performing great feats of physical strength and be amazed at what the human body is capable of doing. But I, too, can perform amazing feats through spiritual power—regardless of my body build or strength.

One way I can exercise spiritual power is through forgiveness. With God as my source and inspiration, I can forgive, which frees me of any hurt feelings or anger.

And if I feel the situation is so overwhelming that I will never be able to forgive, I remember Jesus' example of pure love and forgiveness: He said, "Father, forgive them; for they do not know what they are doing."

With divine vision, I see beyond appearances to the truth of God's wisdom and power in me.

I look beyond appearances to the truth of God's presence.

Day 195

—◆—

*Trusting that larger forces than yourself are at work
in your life, you will give up the demand for the outcome
you think you want and learn to appreciate whatever
it is you get. This is true freedom.*—*Carol Orsborn*

**THE
BIGGER
PICTURE**

I may feel at times that no matter
how hard I try, I just cannot make
things work out the way they should.
Then I know it is time to let go. I let go
and let God work through me to bring order to my
activities.

From time to time, I face challenges that leave me
feeling inadequate or frustrated because I know how
things should be. Letting go gets me past these feelings
and helps me see the bigger picture, one in which God's
order is very present.

So I make letting go a moment-by-moment,
situation-by-situation practice. Beginning with small,
everyday occurrences and including everything that
comes my way, I let go and let God help me out. With
God's help, nothing is impossible for me.

> As I let go and place everything in God's care,
> I begin to see the bigger picture.

Day 196

—◆—

Beloved,

Come to Me, and I will give you rest. Trust in Me, and let Me help you through every situation. When you do, you will find that every moment of your life is filled with wonder, that every moment is a time of golden opportunities.

Look beyond appearances to what you know in your heart is true: We are one! One with Me, you are one with every other creation on Earth. As you live each day in harmony with others, you will begin to see—perhaps for the first time—how powerful unconditional love and faith are in bringing about miracles.

In this glorious moment, we are united in a vision—a vision for the future of what can be achieved through harmony and love.

My blessings are with you as you continue on the grand adventure that is your life!

"Come to me, all you that are weary and are carrying heavy burdens, and I will give you rest."—Matthew 11:28

Day 197

—◆—

*What a wonderful life I've had! I only wish
I'd realized it sooner.*
—Colette Sidonie-Gabrielle

**BLESSED
AWAKENING**
When I look in a mirror, am I always
happy with the person I see looking
back at me? I will be when I am open
to discovering more of the wonder that
is me and understand that I am worthy of all that God
is offering me.

I awaken to the wonder of God and discover
myself—the talents I have, the things that I can
accomplish, and the joy I experience in accomplishing
them. I am confident and always willing to try again, for
I know that God gives me an unlimited number of
chances.

There is wonder in all things and in all situations.
Every experience of my life is an opportunity to learn
more about myself and about giving and receiving
unconditional love.

What I have actually discovered is God. My spiritual
awakening is generated by my faith in God and
enriched by my love for all that God has created.

I awaken to the wonder of God.

DAILY WORD FOR WOMEN

Day 198

◆

*If women learn to be something themselves [and learn]
that the only way to teach is to be fine and shining
examples, we will have in one generation the most
remarkable and glorious children.—Brenda Ueland*

**IN THIS
MOMENT**

When I live in each moment with an
awareness of God, I am infused with
spiritual power and understanding. So
instead of being overwhelmed by
thinking about all that I need to do to reach a goal, I feel
at peace. I can then concentrate on taking one step at a
time toward my goal.

At peace, I choose the goals that are most meaningful
to me. If I need to lose weight, I commit to losing the
first pound of my weight-loss goal, which in turn
inspires me along the way till I reach my ideal weight.

If I am saving for a down payment on a home or for
college tuition, I focus on saving a few dollars at a time,
which continues to close the gap between me and my
goal. Every moment I am aware of God enriches me
and everything I do.

**Aware of God, I am infused with spiritual power
and understanding.**

Day 199

—◆—

There's something about knowing God is part of me. . . .
And I have a lot of confidence in that knowing.
—Susan Ford Bales

BREATH OF LIFE

My healing begins with me—my acceptance of myself as nothing less than a genuine creation of the Creator of life.

My faith is in God—the spirit of God that enlivens every cell of my being. I am alive with the life of God, and I am cared for and nurtured by the spirit of God. I think of and see myself expressing such vitality that I literally glow with life.

Within my chest beats a heart fashioned by the Master Creator. Every thought or word of thanksgiving that I give to God flows through me as peace and joy that inspire me to live life fully.

In prayer, I sweep away any thought, any tendency that would come between me and a total restoration. I am renewed in every moment of life as I breathe deeply of the breath of life.

God is expressing ever-renewing life
through me now.

Day 200

—◆—

I wasn't afraid to fail. Something good
always comes out of failure.
—Anne Baxter

LIFE STORY I am enthusiastic about life because God is my constant companion and guide throughout life. With every thought and action, I cooperate with God in creating a life story that is filled with wonder and discovery.

I see myself as complete and whole. I understand that, in my unfolding story of life, each challenge is an opportunity for me to gain wisdom and strength.

People will come and go in my life, and I am blessed by the love and friendship that I share with them. Yet, God is constant—my unlimited source of wisdom and love. I never feel alone in any situation because I am so aware of God's sweet spirit, which continually encourages and guides me.

I thank God for giving me life and for always helping me to make the most of it.

God is inspiring and guiding me in a life
of wonder and discovery.

Day 201

— ◆ —

Without a goal to work toward,
we will not get there.
—Natasha Josefowitz

INSPIRED BY GOD I would not think of taking a trip or a vacation without first making preparations. Then, because I have already taken care of details, I can give my full attention to enjoying the scenery and my activities.

And there is an even higher order of preparation: spending time with God. Immersing myself in the presence of God has long-lasting results: I feel less stress and do not worry about the little things—things I usually have no control over anyway. I feel more relaxed and prepared to deal with whatever comes my way.

I rely on God's wisdom to guide me. If I encounter an obstacle in the road ahead, I am prepared. I can choose to go around it or I can attempt to remove it. Whatever my decision, it is based on sound judgment and inspired by God.

With God, I am always prepared.

Day 202
———◆———

There is nothing the human heart so longs for,
so cries out after, as to know God.
—H. Emilie Cady

LISTEN In silent communion with God, I listen. I listen and hear a message of wisdom and comfort that directs me and helps me without hesitation through every challenge.

As I listen with my heart and soul, I hear the true message that God has for me—a message of unqualified love and eternal hope, a message of everlasting joy and inner peace. I listen, I hear, and I am receptive to what God is telling me.

And God also listens to me. God understands me and is so completely aware of my needs that I do not worry about using the right words or about how I sound. I just know that God knows and accepts me as I am.

In this holy communion, I place my life, my total being, in God's care. And I know without a doubt that only order and untold blessings will be the result.

In the quiet of prayer, I listen.

DAILY WORD FOR WOMEN

Day 203

—◆—

Beloved,

I have created you from My love. I ask nothing more of you than your faith in Me. Be what I have created you to be—a pure, loving spiritual being. The essence of what I am is within you.

I have breathed the very breath of life into you, life that will sustain and renew your body. Know that healing is yours and claim it.

Never, for even an instant, will I leave you. Listen as My words of wisdom and guidance resonate throughout your being. The answers you seek have been given to you, and as you listen with your mind and your soul, you will know what those answers are. Listen, dear one, and know.

"Know that I am with you
and will keep you wherever you go."
—Genesis 28:15

Day 204

— ◆ —

Every child born into the world is a new thought
of God, an ever-fresh and radiant possibility.
—Kate Douglas Wiggin

TREASURES OF THE HEART

As a child, I may have read stories about explorers sailing the seas and finding sunken treasure. Then I daydreamed about myself going on such an adventure. Perhaps back then, finding priceless treasures seemed possible for me.

I can recapture that same feeling of wonderful possibilities by remembering that treasures of the heart, the greatest treasures I can ever hope to receive, are already within me. My treasure chest contains emotional strength and well-being, endless energy, and even more of God's blessings.

With such treasures of the heart as my own, I believe all things are possible for me. I move forward in fulfilling my hopes and dreams, and I live my life knowing that I am blessed by God—now and forever.

God's treasures await me!

Day 205

—◆—

Winners take chances. Like everyone else, they fear
failing, but they refuse to let fear control them.
—Nancy Simms

A WINNER! Life would be easier if every situation had clearly defined rules, or if I knew in advance the results of my actions and where I stood in relation to everyone and everything. I would feel like a winner then, for I would know that by following the rules, my success was guaranteed.

In reality, few things in life are so simple, and I often have to make choices with which not everyone will agree. This is why it is important for me to look to God for direction. When I follow God's guidance, I will be a winner!

God leads me down paths that help me become more aware of my own spirituality. Then I am more aware of God's presence; and this, above all else, is what truly makes me a winner!

I am a winner!

Day 206

—◆—

Where there is great love
there are always miracles.
—Willa Cather

LOVE EVERLASTING   When I am open to fully experiencing the pure love of God— as I am now—I receive an infusion of strength. The power of divine love allows me to accomplish what I may have felt I could not accomplish only a few moments ago.

Because God's presence is everywhere, I can never be separated from everlasting love or denied the soul-enriching experience of loving God. Divine, pure love is instilled in my heart and cannot be lost or misplaced.

Like a tender sapling stretching to become a mighty oak tree, my love for God continues to grow. Supported by God's love, I can rise above any challenge.

I cannot help but celebrate God's presence as I live a life inspired by the pure joy of being loved and being loving.

I am loved and loving.

Day 207

— ◆ —

Since you get more joy out of giving joy to others,
you should put a good deal of thought into the happiness
that you are able to give.—Eleanor Roosevelt

**JOYFUL
ADVENTURE**

I can feel God's spirit within me,
energizing me and filling me with joy.
At times, my joy may be beneath the
surface of my awareness, but it is
always within me, waiting for me to release it and let
it flow.

My joy of spirit is an unquenchable gladness that
cannot be suppressed, cannot be held down, cannot be
altered by the negative thoughts or feelings or attitudes
of others. I am filled with joy! I am filled with the spirit
of God! I am filled with the life of God!

I let God's joy fill me up and overflow from me as
true joy in living, as happiness and love and excitement
for this adventure called life.

**God's spirit fills me and flows
from me as unquenchable joy.**

Day 208

♦

*I was dreaming with open eyes about a great performance
and I have seen that work can transform the dream
into reality.—Nadia Comaneci*

**DIVINE
ENERGY**

I have faith that the sun will come
up tomorrow. I know from past
experience that the sun is always
shining—even when clouds hide it
from my view.

With even greater assurance, I know that the presence
of God is always with me—even when appearances
seem to suggest otherwise. Faith in God rises up within
me like the morning sun, filling me with the light of
spiritual understanding.

Yes, my faith is in God. So no matter what happens
to me or around me, I am assured of God's eternal,
tender care. The spirit of God is a radiant light that
shines within me and from me as divine energy.

I am filled with the radiant light of divine energy.

Day 209

♦

There are two ways of meeting difficulties: you alter the difficulties or you alter yourself meeting them.
—*Phyllis Bottome*

ALWAYS AN ANSWER

When I have tried everything I can think of to solve a problem and still the solution eludes me, I may be tempted to give up. But I won't give up when I turn to God, because my trust in God reminds me that there is always a way, always a solution to every problem. With God, I won't give up; I go on.

Thinking about God takes my mind off the problem and puts it where it should be—on being open to the solution. In God's presence, I realize that I have the strength to go on, that I can move forward to discover the right answer. And finding the right answer is possible, for God has given me all the resources that I need to find it.

I have patience and courage through any challenge, because I know that with God, there is always a way, always an answer.

With God, there is always a way,
always a solution, always an answer.

Day 210

——◆——

Beloved,

Your life is both a responsibility and a gift that I share with you. And because I love and care for you, I want you to enjoy each day as a blessing.

Accept life as an adventure, for it is. Bless those whom you meet with your loving presence. You are one of My messengers here on Earth, and I ask that you always be an expression of pure, unconditional love.

When you are facing others who may not agree with you, ask yourself what I would encourage you to do. How would I encourage you to act? What words would I guide you to say? Then follow Me and do the things that I lead you to do.

Beloved, there is a sacred bond which unites us, a bond that will withstand any test of time and endure any challenge made upon it. Together we will make your life an adventure to be enjoyed.

"Keep alert, stand firm in your faith,
be courageous, be strong."
—1 Corinthians 16:13

GOD'S GIFT OF LIFE!

BY MAYA BRANDENBERGER

Tests had determined that I was carrying a baby girl and that she would die as soon as she was born. The doctors had told me she would not be able to breathe once she was outside my body.

I had chosen to be in the quiet, peaceful atmosphere of a small country hospital and to be assisted by a midwife. The doctor was there as a friend of the midwife and knew that there was to be no intervention if the baby did not breathe. As the midwife coached me, she suddenly seemed to panic, saying, "You have to keep pushing!" But I just could not stand the thought that I might be pushing my baby out to her death. The doctor looked at me and said, "It's okay. I promised Johanna a kiss if she would breathe."

And Johanna was born alive! She chose to breathe by herself and received the promised kiss from the doctor. That was seven years ago, and this child—who has a major heart-lung condition and a poor immune system—has outlived every dire prediction without hospitalization or surgery. Johanna has a dignity about her that is so natural and powerful that she has radically changed my life. She has truly been a gift of life for everyone who knows her.

Day 211

—◆—

Our faculty of imagination needs to form
a mental picture of the presence of God as being
within us, not a god far off.—Vera Dawson Tait

MY REFUGE

If I were ever caught outside in a downpour of rain, I would just naturally know what to do: I would seek shelter.

I would also seek shelter if I were caught in a difficult situation—not in an attempt to run away from a problem, but from a desire to turn to God's spirit within me. In the shelter of God's presence, I savor the security and understanding I need to experience.

With my full attention on the presence of God, I am at peace. I feel a gratitude that can only come from knowing true security—the peace of God.

I am no longer anxious about what the future may hold because I know that God will be with me, helping me through whatever is there for me to experience.

God is my refuge and my strength.

Day 212

—◆—

Lasting happiness occurs when joy finds
a home within our hearts, and we give ourselves
the freedom to be who we are.—Ardath Rodale

FREE What kind of situations and conditions am I most likely to talk myself into and out of on any given day?

I will be my own best teacher when I use a language which prepares me to expect the best from myself and which inspires me to continue to do my best.

This kind of talk is a language that arises from my soul and encourages me to excel—not in competition with others, but in an eagerness to enrich myself spiritually.

With freedom of spirit, I allow the wisdom of God to speak to me and as me. I invite the courage of God to uphold me and accomplish through me. Like new growth bursting through the earth, I free myself of old limitations and habits. I open myself to the magnificence of God in everyday life.

Using a language of the soul, I allow divine wisdom
to speak to me and through me.

Day 213

— ♦ —

The peace you feel in your heart
makes you a peacemaker.
—Martha Smock

EXPERIENCING PEACE   Peace between people is a state of order and calm that exists as long as all who are involved agree to be peaceful. Inner peace, however, is a serenity of the soul that emanates from the spirit of God within each individual.

Divine peace is always within me, waiting to be experienced as serenity by me. Whenever I bring my awareness to God in prayer, I am consciously connected to the very source of tranquillity.

Once I have experienced divine peace, I understand that it exceeds my greatest expectations and breaks past any preconceived limitations. And I will yearn for the return of it should my thoughts ever go astray.

I experience the peace of God
whenever I experience the presence of God.

Day 214

◆

*All the way to Heaven
is Heaven.*
—Catherine of Sienna

THANK YOU, GOD

Loving Spirit, I am so grateful for Your presence in my life that I am filled to overflowing with thanksgiving!

Thank You, God, for loving me and for strengthening me. Your spirit flows throughout my body and energizes me. Knowing You are with me always, I am uplifted.

God, I am grateful for all the blessings in my life: for cherished friends, for faith and hope, for the nourishing environment in which I live and work.

I am thankful that You have created me to express ever-renewing life. With every beat of my heart, Your love surges through me, and I give thanks.

**In the presence of God, I celebrate a fullness
of joy that breaks forth into thanksgiving!**

Day 215

This life is for awakening to who we are—
co-creators with God. Our dreams are the stepping-stones
to that awakening.—Mary Manin Morrissey

SIMPLY TRUE

When I stop trying to make something happen and just allow myself to be in partnership with God in letting it happen, I am amazed with the results. Obstacles to my goals disappear and doors to opportunities open to me.

What may seem too simple is absolutely true: There is nothing more I need do than to be open to and cooperate with God's presence in order to experience divine wonder in all matters—from daily routines to life-changing events.

I release all to God and remind myself, "I am in partnership with the one power in the universe." As if transported on the wings of spirit, I move from feeling concern to being one with God in creating a life of order and peace.

In partnership with God, I experience
the divine wonder of life.

Day 216

◆

*If you haven't forgiven yourself something,
how can you forgive others?*
—*Delores Hureta*

**RESPONDING
WITH LOVE** Forgiveness is an activity by which the spirit of God gently moves me past hurts and disappointments and on to serenity and fulfillment. So instead of relying on limited reasoning or emotional reactions, I respond to others with love and compassion.

I may never know for sure who benefits most from my being forgiving—myself or others—but I do know that giving to others from the spirit of God within me blesses me. I feel better immediately when loving, caring thoughts and words have replaced any angry thoughts or unpleasant memories.

The most enriching experience from forgiveness is that I gain a greater understanding of myself as a spiritual being. I feel the presence of God as the love and gentleness in the forgiveness I give—to myself and others.

**The love and understanding I give flow from
the spirit of God within me.**

Day 217

—◆—

Beloved,

Every time you turn to Me, know in your heart that I welcome you. The security you feel when you are aware of Me is there for you at all times, but you resonate with the truth of it as you speak to Me in a language of the soul.

Each time you let the peace that I am rise up within you to bathe you in a warm glow of serenity, you are thankful. And I want you to know that I am thankful for you, for your every word and act in partnership with Me.

You may not see the glow of love on your face as you forgive, but those who receive your forgiveness and understanding do. And I, too, behold the beauty of your soul when you are aglow with love and forgiveness. What a beautiful light you are in the world!

"God is our refuge and strength."
—Psalm 46:1

Day 218

—◆—

My life has been a tapestry of rich and royal hue,
an everlasting vision of the ever changing view.
—Carole King

CLEAR VISION When I am inspired by creative ideas or a clear vision of a goal, the reality of what I want to achieve seems to develop so effortlessly.

Maybe this is because such a vision is a wake-up call from Spirit so that I will not miss some blessing. So I know that holding a picture in mind of the education, the employment, or the relationship I desire is continually alerting me to cooperate with making it a reality.

Certainly my prayer times are important in holding to a clear vision and in making adjustments in my perception. With a clear vision, I know what satisfies my soul, and I do not make the mistake of settling for less. My greatest soul satisfaction at any time is in knowing the presence of God—in quiet moments and in celebrations of my heart.

My clear vision prepares me for a divine reality.

Day 219

——◆——

*The awakening of consciousness is not unlike
the crossing of a frontier—one step and you are
in another country.—Adrienne Rich*

**ONE STEP
AT A
TIME**
A plan becomes a reality only after
the first action step is taken. If I doubt
my own ability to carry through with a
desire, I might hesitate or never even
begin to pursue it.

So each time I begin a project, I picture myself
mentally taking one step at a time to complete it. As I
take the first step, I remind myself that all is in divine
order. Then I take another step, this time with a greater
feeling of security. As I continue forward with each
progressive step, I gain momentum and my trust builds
to new heights.

I know that God is in charge, so with each step, I am
moving forward in faith. I can meet any challenge and
accomplish whatever needs to be done by me.

**Yes, it is true: I am stepping forward in faith
and bringing my plans into reality!**

Day 220

◆

The life of the spirit requires less and less;
time is ample and its passing sweet.
—Annie Dillard

GOD'S RADIANT LIGHT

When I ask God for guidance, I am not looking for an easy answer or for a way out of having to make my own decisions. Rather, I am asking God to guide the decisions I make so that they will bring about what is best for me and for everyone concerned.

So I seek God in silence, and God answers. In silence, I become aware of my oneness with God and with God's radiant light—a light of understanding which shines so brightly that its warm glow infuses me with confidence and serenity.

Enfolded in God's light, I can literally feel the darkness of doubt or confusion being gently swept away. In its place is a peace like none I have ever before experienced.

God's radiant light bathes me
in a warm glow of confidence and serenity.

Day 221

The universe would not
be complete without you.
—Mary-Alice Jafolla

**DIAMOND
IN THE
ROUGH**
A diamond in the rough bears little resemblance to the polished and beautiful stone it will eventually become. Yet it is essentially the same stone, just waiting for the master's touch to bring out its inner shine.

Like the unpolished stone, I am filled with a natural beauty and light. And as I trust in God's spirit within, I learn to value inner light—the spiritual identity of myself and others.

Through grace, God has given me all I could ever need to live up to my divine potential. And through grace, I am gently and lovingly guided in using the unique talents and abilities that God has given me.

As I share my gifts with others, I let my inner light shine more brightly.

Inner light shines from me as my spiritual identity.

Day 222

◆

When you respond to something because it's
so beautiful, you're really looking at the soul of
the person who made it.—Alice Walker

WORK OF ART

Every day is a new day in which I can be renewed by my own acceptance of the truth about myself.

I am a work of art by the Master Creator. Granted, I may not always live up to my full potential, but I don't mistake any longing to be more as disappointment in what I have achieved. I simply know that the greatness of God within me is ready to come forward. As a creation of God, there is always something greater—something that is waiting within me to be, something that is more than I have ever before been.

Even with the things I think I have mastered, I may find that I have a bit more to learn and achieve. And, oh, the rewards of being a more committed spouse, a more involved parent, a more resourceful employee! Best of all, I become more aware of God.

I am a work of art, created by God.

Day 223

◆

If you stop to be kind, you must
swerve often from your path.
—*Mary Webb*

DIVINE PLAN

Throughout my life I will play many roles. My role could be as a student, a professional, a spouse and parent, or a retiree.

Yet no matter where I am in my life's journey, I probably have had to take a detour or two along the way. And what I have discovered is this: Out of unplanned events and apparent disorder come some of my most rewarding experiences.

I have learned that I am stronger, wiser, and more patient than I ever dreamed I could be. And most importantly, I have learned that God has something better in store for me than I could ever imagine on my own.

Now I understand that my best plan in life is to be prepared to accept the wonderful possibilities of a divine plan.

I accept all the wonderful possibilities
of God's divine plan.

Day 224

◆

Beloved,

Do you realize how magnificent you are? I have given you a spirit of eternal life, so let the beauty of your true self come forth. Your radiance is a reflection of a sacredness within you. Together we can dispel any hint of darkness or despair from your life.

Know that My healing life renews you from the inside out. With each day that passes, you build on an understanding of the perfection that is within you waiting to show forth. The experiences of your life are a process that calls more and more of your inner perfection to be lived in your life—giving a finishing touch to the master work that you are.

Moment by moment, day by day, My plan is unfolding within you. Let it come forth, and see your dreams come true!

"Everything old has passed away;
see, everything has become new!"
—2 Corinthians 5:17

Day 225

—◆—

If you let yourself be absorbed completely, if you surrender completely to the moments as they pass, you live more richly those moments.—Anne Morrow Lindbergh

SWEET SURRENDER   Have I ever left for a vacation or another trip with only a few pieces of luggage and found that when I returned home I had far more than what I had originally taken with me?

The same may be true of my life experiences. I start a new day or a new relationship with a positive outlook, only to find that as I continue on, I take on excess emotional baggage that weighs me down.

I can lighten my load by releasing the burden of negative memories and emotions in sweet surrender. In their place, I welcome golden thoughts of the peace and love that can only come from God. Because I desire to have more of God in my life, I radiate more of the spirit of God within me out into my world.

In sweet surrender, I release all into God's care.

Day 226

—◆—

*Our words of healing turn on the generator . . . we feel
a new, buoyant lightness coupled with fresh strength.*
—*Mary Katherine MacDougall*

**VIBRANT
BEING**

To be the vibrantly alive person God created me to be, I think thoughts of health and healing. I speak words of life and vitality to myself and about myself.

Such incredible power is released through words of life and healing. They resonate through my entire being, evoking a response that awakens me to living life fully.

Healing words encourage me to be aware of God as the source of life, and as I let such encouragement saturate my mind and body, I am empowered.

The life within the cells of my body responds to my thoughts and words. So I think and speak of life, and then I just naturally move forward by doing what enriches me spiritually, emotionally, and physically.

**"Yes" is the response of my cells to words
of life and healing.**

Day 227

—◆—

Peace has to be created in order to be maintained.
It is the product of faith, strength, energy, will, sympathy,
justice, imagination, and the triumph of principle.
—Dorothy Thompson

WELLSPRING OF PEACE God, I delight in Your divine plan of inner peace. Tapping into an internal wellspring of peace, I experience the love and support You are constantly pouring out to me.

A silent yet powerful message of peace emanates from Your spirit within me. And when I listen and then let myself be saturated with divine peace, I realize a serenity greater than any I have ever before imagined I could know.

In every situation I have gone through, God, You were with me. In every circumstance I will go through, You will be with me. You are with me now—quieting my thoughts and soothing my body. Your peace tenderly moves throughout my being, healing and restoring me. Enfolded in Your peace, I am serene and confident.

I am serene and confident, because I know
that God is my constant source of peace.

Day 228

---◆---

When we escaped from Cuba,
all we could carry was our education.
—Alicia Coro

LEARN

If I could play a video of my early life, I would see the incredible investment I have made in learning to read. This investment has opened up a whole new world of knowledge to me.

And the wonder of it all is that God created me to learn. I have been given a magnificent tool—a brain—and an invincible spirit—God's spirit within me—that allow me to increase my knowledge and to have true peace and soul satisfaction as I learn.

Every day there is something new to learn. If I am preparing for or taking a test, I relax and know that God has created me to learn and to give expression to what I have learned. It is not a matter of if I can learn; it is a matter of releasing all tension and concern so that I do learn.

I relax and know the truth about myself:
God has created me to learn.

Day 229

—◆—

Everyone has talent. What is rare is
the courage to follow talent to the dark place
where it leads.—Erica Jong

THE GREATNESS WITHIN Whether I am cleaning the garage or the living room in my home, I turn up the lights. This way I will be certain to clean thoroughly into every corner and clear away all the trash. When I clean again, I won't have to deal with an accumulation of dirt.

The same is true when I consider freeing my mind of any situation from the past that has lingered in my thoughts or might be keeping me from enjoying life now. I use my freedom of spirit to illumine my mind and heart so that I can seek out those limitations and free myself of them.

The spirit of God within me is far greater than any negative thought. Through the power of spirit, I examine my life and find that I am capable of fulfilling my hopes and dreams. I am eager to begin a new day.

I help create a new me by expressing the greatness of God that is within me.

Day 230

◆

The soul should always stand ajar,
ready to welcome the ecstatic experience.
—Emily Dickinson

SOUL ENRICHMENT The enrichment of my life begins within me. As I recognize and release an inner spark of spirit, I am enthused about being totally alive in spirit, mind, and body.

I now realize that the yearning I might not have recognized before is for the unconditional love of God, the infallible wisdom of God, the all-pervading presence of God.

I know that nothing could bless me more than knowing God and knowing that the spirit of God lives within me, moves through me and out from me as love and wisdom, energy and assurance.

Yes, God is the source of all that enriches me and my life. I give thanks for the people, the comfort, and the financial security I enjoy. But I also know that God is the creator of all people, the source of all that is eternal and fulfilling.

God is the source of all that enriches me and my life.

Day 231

—◆—

Beloved,

You are a vibrant, energetic, brimming-with-life expression of My spirit. With every breath you take and every beat of your heart, I am blessing you with life.

As you let go of worries and fears and give yourself in sweet surrender to Me, you make a conscious connection with My presence. Now let yourself be filled with peace, let Me give you a peace that enriches your soul.

Every experience in your life is a learning experience, for in everything you do you are learning about the divinity within you. Reach out with your mind and your heart and touch the divinity within others, for you are all one—important members of My universal family of love.

"I delight to do your will, O my God;
your law is within my heart."
—Psalm 40:8

DAILY WORD FOR WOMEN

Day 232

— ◆ —

To love deeply in one direction makes us
more loving in all others.
—Madame Swetchine

GOLDEN RULE When I am with family and friends, co-workers, or even strangers, I make choices about the way I interact with them. One of the most important choices I can make is to live and work in harmony with others.

If someone says or does something that I do not agree with, I remember that I was created by the God of love to be loving. Then I am courteous and respectful to all people.

A friendly manner goes a long way in establishing a harmonious environment and good relationships. So I live by the Golden Rule and treat others with the same acceptance as I would like them to treat me.

My awareness of the presence of God within me and within others prompts me to create a peace-filled environment that nourishes all my relationships.

I can and do help create the peace-filled
environment in which I live.

Day 233

---◆---

We do not need to pray to God for light; we need only
to pray for awareness, awareness of the sure
and shining light of Spirit at the heart of our being.
—*Martha Smock*

S T O P ,
L O O K ,
A N D
L I S T E N The human eyes and ears are
intricately fashioned receptors of an
untold number of sights and sounds.
So throughout the day, I take time to
stop what I am doing and then look and listen to what
God has to show me.

I listen to the sounds of God around me in nature:
How relaxing it feels to listen to the gentle sound of the
wind whispering through the leaves of the trees.

I look with awe at the sights of God: The people I see
are beautiful creations, each one different and yet the
same in spirit. We are all created in the divine image.

Today and every day, I take time to stop, look, and
listen to the sights and sounds of God's presence.

I stop, look, and listen to the sights
and sounds of God.

Day 234

—◆—

You can choose to climb your mountain alone
or you can choose to climb it with God.
—Deborah L. Cameron

SPIRITUAL BEING

It takes a lot of energy and determination to climb a mountain. When the top is finally reached, the exhilaration of achievement will have made it all worthwhile.

And I have had emotional mountaintop experiences—the exhilaration of achieving some goal or realization. Or, having gone through a time of challenge, I find that I feel both at peace and energized when things finally do smooth out.

Yet, even higher than the physical and emotional exhilaration I enjoy, there is the mountaintop experience of realizing my own spirituality. This is when I cease to struggle on my own and let the power of God within me work through me. Then I soar above any confusion around me and discover the true joy of living as a spiritually empowered being.

**I have discovered the exhilaration
of living as a spiritual being.**

Day 235

—◆—

*I'll always remember the time my father turned
to me with tears in his eyes and told me that the greatest
gift I had given him was teaching my children to pray.*
—Pauletta Washington

HONORING YOU When I think about all the people who have enriched my life, I feel a great desire to bless and honor them, and I can—in my prayers for each and every one of them.

I give thanks to God for my dear ones. I honor them for all that they are and all that they do. Most of all, I appreciate my loved ones for being unique and wonderful expressions of God's sacred spirit.

I picture my loved ones glowing with the light of God, radiating love and joy to all who are willing to receive. I give thanks for the wonderful, positive influence both friends and family alike have been for me. I love them and honor them for the sacred beings they are.

**I honor God when I honor my loved ones
as sacred beings.**

Day 236

It is when you are really living in the present—working, thinking, lost, absorbed in something you care about very much—that you are living spiritually.
—Brenda Ueland

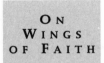

On Wings of Faith

Thank You, God, for life! I know that in all my experiences—whether they are joyous or emotionally painful—You are there to love and comfort me, to be my strength.

When my burdens seem too great, You lift me to new heights, and I am able to soar on wings of faith. When the path before me is dark and I am uncertain, You are the light that shines before me to guide my way. When I am not sure if I have true love in my life, You give me love that is far greater than any I have ever experienced.

When the world seems full of discord and strife, You encourage me to make a difference by being peaceful myself and then allowing my peace to flow out from me into the lives of others. God, You are my strength.

God is my strength.

Day 237

—◆—

As you pray and attune yourself wholly to God,
you begin to notice that you are more loving, more joyful.
—Peggy Pifer

THE SOUND OF SILENCE

When I become quiet and listen in silence, a gentle, hushed voice beckons me: "Come, enter into a realm of peace and tranquillity."

I hear the sound of silence as an invitation to be totally one with God. Immersed in the presence of God, I receive the answers I seek, the guidance I long for, and the hope that springs eternal.

In silence, I am immersed in a oneness with God. I understand that God loves me and loves through me—forever.

Within silence is the sound of pure, unconditional love being given and received. In the presence of God, I release any thought of regrets, past hurts, or shame. In return I receive peace, tranquillity, and the assurance that I am a masterpiece created by the Master.

In silence, I am totally immersed in the presence of God.

Day 238

—◆—

Beloved,

Allow yourself to live each day in My light and love. When situations cause uncertainty or doubt in your mind, ask yourself, "Why am I thinking such thoughts?"

When you are fully in My presence, you will discover that you do not worry about anything because doubt does not exist in My presence. So leave your fears at the doorstep of your soul and enter into a sanctuary of peace.

In My presence, all things are possible, for you are one with true reality. No situation or person can harm you, for only love can exist in the silence of your soul.

Remember that even when there seems to be darkness, light still exists. All you need do is look within your soul, for I am there.

"Remember that it is not you that support the root, but the root that supports you."
—Romans 11:18

Day 239

---◆---

When we pray, mighty forces move. Prayer helps us overcome life's obstacles. It helps give us peace of mind, and helps us find our own strength.
—Rosemary Ellen Guiley

UNLIMITED POSSIBILITIES

This very moment is brimming with possibilities—possibilities for new understanding, new growth, and new blessings for me. Even when it seems that one challenge after another comes to me, I know that each one is a new opportunity to learn about myself and the world around me. So instead of focusing on the challenge, I look for the possibilities that it offers.

With God, everything is possible—even the seemingly impossible. Yet it is up to me to look beyond what appears to be and see what really is—and that is God: God in me and God in everything around me.

From this perspective, I begin to see that every moment truly is filled with possibilities—the endless possibilities that only God can provide.

Every moment of every day is brimming with unlimited possibilities!

Day 240

— ◆ —

You live through the darkness from
what you learned in the light.
—Hope MacDonald

LET GO,
LET GOD

Responsibilities can leave me feeling overwhelmed at times. So I slow down, take a deep breath, and let go of concern. No matter what is facing me right now, God is with me, and I know that together God and I will make it through.

I let go of worries because I know that worrying will not relieve me of my responsibilities. I let go of doubts about myself and others because I know that God is in charge. I let go of fears about what the future may hold because I know that there is nothing more powerful than God's mighty presence. With God, I have nothing to fear.

God is my partner, my guide, my true source of inspiration. God blesses me so, and by letting go of worry and letting God guide me, I am opening myself to even greater blessings.

I let go and I let God.

THE GIFT OF GOD'S LOVE
BY LYNNE BROWN

I stood in the doorway, watching through tear-filled eyes as my three-year-old daughter left with her grandparents. I was about to deliver a baby soon, and my parents offered to take Jessica home with them for the night.

The tears that ran down my cheeks were from a question in my heart: I felt such joy for the new life I was carrying, but I also wondered if I could love my second-born as much as I loved Jessica.

And then, as I silently prayed, I felt in the depths of my soul what my mind already knew: God's everlasting and unconditional love is for all and in all. Through the spirit of God within me, I was capable of expressing love to 2 or 200 children!

Our son, Zachary, was born early the next morning. The moment he arrived and was placed in my arms, I felt a tremendous love for him—love that was full and complete. And my love for Jessica was in no way lessened; it has grown. I give thanks for Jessica and Zachary, and for the gift of God's love that is given to me and expressed through me.

Day 241

—◆—

*I like to compare prayer to the wind. You cannot
actually see the wind, but you can see the results of it.
—Rosalind Rinker*

**NEW
SEASON**

Just as there are different seasons
of the year, there are also different
seasons of my life.

Occasionally a season may be one
of growth in which I have such a spurt of energy and
creativity that I accomplish much. Another season of
my life is one of rest and dormancy. I am quiet and
contemplative, and nothing appears to be happening
with me or through me.

What I realize from the changing seasons is that a
time of rest is just as important as a time of activity. In a
time of quiet, I am preparing to do more and be more. I
am consciously connecting with the spirit of God
within me. And out of this season of spiritual
awareness, a new me emerges.

**This is a new season of spiritual
awareness for me.**

Day 242

—◆—

We can think of grace as God's love, God's life,
God's wisdom, all that God is, being given to us freely,
unconditionally, and automatically.
—Debbie K. Bryan

A
S A C R E D
G I F T

Grace is divine love actively working for me in every moment. Although most of the time I am not aware of it, divine grace is continually blessing me and bringing order into my life.

Each day is a new beginning—a fresh start—so I do not become caught up in regret about what I have or have not done in the past. I accept the guidance I receive to move forward as an indication that it is time to leave any doubts behind. I open my arms and my life to grace and give thanks for the love of God that is within me and enfolding me.

God is always with me, so divine grace is always with me, too. Through God's grace, I am inspired to live a life in which I share the love of God with others.

I give thanks for grace, a sacred gift from God.

Day 243

—◆—

The windows of your soul open more fully to the wisdom and inspiration of God when you take time to pray.
—*Sharon S. King*

POSITIVE OUTLOOK Is it always possible to have a positive attitude and still be realistic? Yes, it is!

Can I expect the best in myself and others without setting standards that are impossible to reach? Of course I can, for God's spirit is within me. With God, the possibilities are unlimited.

With faith in God and in myself, I can accomplish great things. By expecting the best in any given situation, I am preparing myself for positive and satisfying experiences.

When I expect the best, I am willing to go the extra mile to achieve the best results. And by expecting the best, I am saying "Yes!" to all the blessings I know are coming my way!

> **I expect the best and say "yes" to all the blessings coming to me today.**

Day 244

——◆——

*When people attend my one-woman stand-up routine,
they feel really good after an hour of laughing. And I get
the greatest lift in the world.—Phyllis Diller*

**JOYFUL
CELEBRATION**
Just thinking back to a time when I felt great joy brings a smile to my lips. A sweet memory sparks a gladness of the soul, an emotional and physical response that lifts me up even when I am feeling down.

I am energized by the joy I feel when I think of the future, anticipating a time when a dream or goal might become a reality. I am ready to move on when only a moment before I may have felt less than enthusiastic about anything.

And what about the joy in the present? When I live the joy of God—the joy of my spiritual identity—my thoughts are whispers of gladness that keep me positive and focused on celebrating my own spiritual identity and the spirituality of all others.

**The joy of God lives through me as a celebration
of my spirituality.**

Day 245

Beloved,

In your times of prayer, you have come to Me for solutions to what is challenging you. Yet you may wonder how to know if a thought, an idea, or a plan is a divine solution.

The answer is quite simple: You will know in the depths of your soul that the guidance you receive is perfect for you. You will know because you receive confirmation from your heart and soul.

My love—divine love—dwells within you. When I speak to you, your faith will answer with a resounding "Yes!"

Because you are first and foremost a spiritual being, you desire to be pure love and understanding. Aware that My peace resides within you, you will never settle for anything less than the serenity that fills your soul.

"He touched their eyes and said,
'According to your faith let it be done
to you.' And their eyes were opened."
—Matthew 9:29–30

Day 246

———◆———

To live sacred lives requires that we live
at the edge of what we do not know.
—Anne Hillman

TRUSTING GOD   I may find it much easier to talk about forgiveness as a way of expressing God's love than to put forgiveness into practice.

Sometimes the people I love the most can cause me the most pain. Perhaps they are not aware that something they have said or done has caused me emotional pain.

I may never understand what motivates the actions of others, but what I do know is this: God loves me and will help me work through every feeling of loss or betrayal.

Trusting in God, I realize that I can forgive—if not their actions, then certainly the people themselves.

God's spirit lives within me and the ones I love. And through forgiveness, I let God's healing light shine through.

As I forgive, I release a flow of God's
healing love out to others.

Day 247

---◆---

We couldn't conceive of a miracle
if none had ever happened.
—Libbie Fudim

WISDOM OF GOD
Even the most well-intentioned advice I have been given may not be right for me. What do I do? I listen courteously, thank the person, and then try to figure out another way.

And there is a better way: With God, I need never doubt that the guidance and inspiration I receive is right for me. It is right for me because God knows me better than I know myself.

So if I am unsure about what to do, I remind myself that the wisdom of God is within me. As I bring it forth in prayer, I shine the light of understanding on every area of my life.

In God's light, I comprehend every situation with a new clarity. I feel a certainty about what is right for me. Living in God's light, I will never be led astray.

The light of God's wisdom is shining brightly
and continually within me.

Day 248

—◆—

Faith is like radar that sees through the fog—the reality of things at a distance that the human eye cannot see.
—Corrie Ten Boom

FAITH IS A BRIDGE My faith in God is a powerful spiritual belief that rushes in to soothe any fears so that I think and act with calmness and wisdom.

And my faith in God is continually growing, for it opens my soul to the wonder of God that is everywhere—in people, events, and circumstances.

There is nothing that God cannot do through me and through others. Because I believe this is so, I am lifted above limitations and obstacles. Faith in God moves me forward and brings me through any and every situation.

Faith is a bridge over which I cross any trouble or challenge to the healing, prosperity, and fulfillment of my dreams. I believe in God, and I know that God also believes in me.

Faith opens my soul to the wonder of God.

Day 249

---◆---

The ways of answered prayer for healing are
as infinite as God is infinite.
—Mary L. Kupferle

WELLSPRING OF LIFE

I may be more aware of God's healing life when I have a need for healing or when someone I love is going through a health challenge.

Yet I know that the life and energy of God are always active within me and within the ones I love, bringing about healing. What my awareness of God does is to keep me cooperating with my own healing. At anytime, I can tap into the wellspring of life within to find the strength and energy I need.

The life of God fills me through and through! From the top of my head to the tips of my toes, divine life surges through my body, renewing and restoring me. Alive with the life of God, I say, "Thank You, thank You, God! I am energized, I am whole, I am well, I am healed!"

The life of God within heals me
and gives me strength.

Day 250

—◆—

We need not be forced to seek Truth by some harsh
experience in life, but we can start now through prayer
and meditation to put our lives and our thoughts in order.
—Connie Fillmore Bazzy

**HIGHER
ORDER**

Before a huge ocean liner can be what it was designed to be—transportation for people and cargo across the widest, deepest expanses of an ocean—it must be launched into the waters. There is a simple, logical order in the ship being in the ocean.

And there is an even higher order—divine order—that supports me in being who I was created to be. So I remember to move myself into the divine order that is always there for me.

How do I do this—especially when my life seems to be in disorder? Well, I know that as I bring myself to a greater awareness of God, I automatically enhance my awareness of the divine order that surrounds and upholds me. I then know I am being who I was created to be: a divine creation in a world of God's order.

**I live in a world of God's order as
a peace-filled creation of God.**

Day 251

—◆—

The light that we want is not some thing
that God has to give; it is God.
—H. Emilie Cady

NEW OPPORTU-NITIES If I am starting a new venture, entering a new relationship, or considering whether to make a change in my life, I may hesitate and wonder if I am doing the right thing. However, I am confident when I include God's guidance in every decision I make.

I do not worry about making a mistake, for God is guiding me. And even if I should make an error in judgment, I can learn from it and do something differently in the future. I am never a failure to God, and when I remember this truth and live it in my life, I am able to relax and enjoy the blessings that await me.

Living a life that is blessed by the grace of God, I joyfully embrace the wonderful opportunities that are unfolding before me today.

Spirit guides me to fresh, new opportunities.

Day 252

—◆—

Beloved,
    You have not always taken the easy way or the smooth road, but every challenge, every success along the way has brought out more of your spiritual nature.
    Your journey continues, but you understand that the miracles you thought were reserved for a few are daily blessings that I give to all. There will never be a day when I am not pouring out My love and peace to you.
    You radiate with life—even in the times when you are most challenged. Remember that I will provide you with bridges over troubles, and remember also that your courage will allow you to cross over to safe ground. You are making steady progress on your life's journey.
    I will comfort you in your times of greatest pain and celebrate with you in your times of greatest joy.

"Do not fear, for I am with you, do not be afraid, for I am your God."
—Isaiah 41:10

Day 253

—◆—

All that is worth cherishing in this world
begins in the heart, not the head.
—Suzanne Chazin

GIVING
LOVE

Some people help others quietly and without any desire for recognition. They give a gentle touch, have intuitive understanding of others' needs, and express compassion without fanfare or effort.

Surely it is love—love for God and for humankind—that inspires them to be caregivers. They see others as the individual creations of God that they really are. They see each physical body as the visible form that has as its center invisible spirit.

In some capacity or another, all people are caregivers. So I want to know that I, too, am giving from the love of God within me. The love I give to others first flows through me to strengthen and inspire me. What better gift could I give to others than the very love out of which all life has been created?

I give the gift of love.

Day 254

—◆—

The opening of your mind, heart, and life to the guidance of spirit is the beginning, not the end, of wisdom.—Martha Smock

RIGHT TRACK Whenever I use a compass correctly, I will stay on the right track and not become lost. But what happens when I feel spiritually or emotionally lost, when I feel as if I am merely wandering through life?

I find my direction by allowing God to show me the way. I do this by releasing every doubt about finding the way and then inviting the spirit of God to work through me.

When I allow myself to be on a divine course, I will always be on the right track. Every day I will find that there is a reason for being where I am and for learning the lessons in life which I am learning.

So as I trust God to show me that way, I know that I am on the right track and living a spiritually enriching life.

With God as my guide, I am on the right track and my way is clear.

Day 255

— ◆ —

*The new growth in the plant swelling against
the sheath, which at the same time imprisons
and protects it, must still be the truest type of progress.*
—Jane Addams

HARVEST Farmers know that before they reap a rich harvest, they must first plant seed and then care for their growing crops. They know that this process does not happen overnight. It takes time and patience.

I, too, give special attention to the blessings I wish to harvest, for the blessings I want most are ones such as love and understanding, health and well-being— blessings that will last a lifetime.

These and other blessings require time to take root and grow and mature in me and in others. The nourishment for these seed-blessings comes from the eternal spirit of life within. And then, in a time of harvest, the beauty of God's spirit shows forth as expressions of life, love, and goodwill.

God provides a glorious harvest of blessings.

Day 256

———◆———

Normal day, let me be aware
of the treasure you are.
—Mary Jean Irion

LIVING
IN THE
LIGHT

I am—right now—living in the pure light and love of God. In fact, I can never be denied God's wisdom and love because I can never be separated from the presence of God.

And it is from this total awareness of God that I pray: "God, I recognize that You are the one presence and power in my life and in all the universe. I have complete faith in You.

"God, You continually bless me. Your gifts of life and breath could never be bought or earned by me, and I do not take even one gift for granted. I have faith that my needs will be met according to Your divine plan.

"God, thank You. Even when I feel that my words of thanks can never be enough, I thank You by living in Your light and love and by sharing Your gifts with the world."

Living in the light and love of God,
I am continually blessed.

Day 257

—◆—

Why should we all dress after the same fashion?
The frost never paints my windows twice alike.
—*Lydia Maria Child*

EVOLVING SOUL

Life is a journey that has its share of twists and turns. I am making progress, though, and reaching new mile markers that will get me to where I need to be. Each day brings new growth and a new understanding of the world around me.

Along the way, I have grown and my appearance has changed. And my perception of myself, my world, and the people around me has changed as well—thought by thought.

When I look at people, I can see their beauty and appreciate the diversity that makes each one unique. That beauty is in me, too, for it is a reflection of the soul—a divine connection with God.

Each day is a forward journey of the soul, a journey that brings a greater awareness of the eternal spirit of life that resides within.

My mind and body give expression
to the beauty of my soul.

Day 258

— ◆ —

As a tree lifts for the sun, so do you
reach up toward God.
—Stella Terrill Mann

LOVING PRESENCE

Throughout my life, the reasons why I seek comfort may vary, but where I find strength and assurance will not—I always find comfort in the presence of God.

Through my prayers and quiet talks with God, I am comforted. And it is in my times of prayer that I am guided to live my life fully and completely in oneness with Spirit. I am totally alert to God and to the actions this realization prompts in me. I am immersed in the comfort and care of God. I have divine reassurance at all times and in all ways.

Just as my physical body needs a constant supply of nourishment to function properly, my spirit needs the nourishment of prayer to be fulfilled. And it is nourished by the living, loving presence of God within me and within every situation in life.

Through the living, loving presence of God,
I am comforted.

Day 259

—◆—

Beloved,

Know that wherever you go, I will go with you. Know, too, that My love is the strong foundation on which you can build your life and your relationships. You have only to trust and let My love live through you.

Hour by hour, day by day, you are expressing more and more of My love into the world. Moment by moment, you are following a course that will bring you to a greater understanding of the miracle-working power of love.

My love within you will increase as you give it expression in everything you do. As you do, know that you are living from your magnificent, spiritual nature.

"According to the grace of God given to me, like a skilled master builder I laid a foundation."
—1 Corinthians 3:10

Day 260

— ◆ —

Listen to the faith of God. God knows things are
not going to come to a sudden end, that life cannot die.
God is not afraid of tomorrow.
—*Vera Dawson Tait*

SPIRIT
OF LIFE
God created my body with
everything it needs to heal itself
naturally. And God also gave me a
"spark of divinity"—the spirit of life
within—as my source of renewal.

However, suddenly or over a period of time,
something may happen that interferes with the natural
healing process. What do I do if this happens to me?
First of all, I never think of myself as less than a creation
of the original, divine plan. I let my words and thoughts
call forth the healing from within me. The health and
well-being I accept in thought is a step forward in
healing.

As I say, "Thank You, God; I am healed now!" I
acknowledge that the spirit of life is radiating
throughout my body, healing and renewing me.

The spirit of life heals me now.

Day 261

—◆—

*Peace is an awareness of the within
as well as the without.*
—Sue Sikking

RADIATE SERENITY   When I think of God's presence around me, I relax and allow myself to be enfolded in a blanket of peace.

Yet when I take my thoughts deeper, to God's presence within me, I know how it feels to radiate serenity. I feel all the tension in my body melting away. I let my thoughts of God's spirit within consciously connect me with the inner peace that is always there for me to experience.

The gentle yet powerful inner peace within me reaches out from me to others. My calm response to a crying child, a tense spouse, or an impatient friend soothes them and prepares the way for peaceful communication and relations.

Wherever I am, I am in the presence of God and divine peace.

**My thoughts of God's presence within lead me
to a realization of peace.**

Day 262

—◆—

If only we'd stop trying to be happy,
we'd have a pretty good time.
—Edith Wharton

I AM JOY

Joy is an integral part of who I am—I am joy! I am life! I am love! I am a celebration of the very spirit of God within me, and it is in my nature to express joy!

I feel joy in many ways but most especially when I allow God to love through me. God's love fills my heart and bubbles up from within in a joyous celebration of the divine spirit that created me.

I also feel joy as life—God-life that is the very essence of my being. Divine life surges through every atom, every cell of my being as a joyous expression of pure energy and life.

When I express joy, I am taking part in a true celebration of God's spirit within.

My joy is a celebration of the spirit
of God within me.

Day 263

—◆—

*You have to be willing to step out of the pack
and take risks, even jump completely out of your element
if that's what it takes.—Carol Bartz*

I WILL FOLLOW

God, I am willing to follow where You guide me, and when I do, I discover a whole new world of wonder to explore.

And, God, what I know and feel to the depths of my soul is this: I am willing to follow You. Out of the seemingly invisible realm of faith, new life opens to me. Assurance replaces regret. Joy overcomes sorrow. Vitality erases fatigue.

With love and power, You have created life from the smallest to the grandest scale. And my heart soars with appreciation when I consider that I am important and needed in Your world of creation.

God, how can I be anything but willing to follow? I know that on any path You lead me, I will discover even more of the glory and wonder You have created.

God, I am willing.

Day 264

♦

Dreams pass into the reality of action. From the action stems the dreams again; and this interdependence produces the highest form of living.
—Anaïs Nin

SHARE THE VISION I have a vision of how the world can be: People of all races and creeds are living in harmony. They realize that although they may have different personal beliefs or may be separated by great distances, they are still one with God.

The natural resources that God has provided for all are being shared in my vision. In this perfect picture, all people have learned to share and give freely of themselves and their talents.

I have a vision, and I know that this dream will be realized, for God is actively at work in my life and in the lives of each person on Earth. We are coming together as one world, one people, one family of God united in a common purpose—to love one another. And out of that love, we respect our differences.

We are one in spirit.

Day 265

◆

Grace has nothing to do with anything that anyone else has ever done. . . . Grace is an inner realization that we are already one with God—always have been and always will be.—Margaret Ponders

SWEET ASSURANCE Beloved Spirit, I see Your beauty and majesty all around me. The sweet assurance of Your eternal love and grace are all I need, and that realization has been fulfilled beyond my expectations.

O sweet Spirit, Your love guides me, Your life heals me, and Your presence nourishes my body and soul. Your grace is a gift that I will cherish forever.

Joy, peace, love, comfort—they are all included in Your grace. My greatest hope is that all people will know the power and magnitude of Your grace and receive the same comfort and rest I have in knowing the blessing of Your presence. I am filled to overflowing with thanksgiving and gratitude.

Sweet Spirit, I am blessed by Your grace.

Day 266

---◆---

Beloved,

You are a great joy to Me, for through you My joy finds expression! So let My joy come forth from within you with every word you speak, with every kind act you extend toward another!

You radiate the love that lives within you. Follow the sure guidance of this love and know that you cannot fail in your efforts to bring more peace and joy and understanding to your surroundings.

As you give to others from your divine nature, you will feel My assurance encouraging you.

Rest assured that whenever you need Me, all you have to do is call. My answer will be an outpouring of My love.

"You hold my right hand."
—Psalm 73:23

Day 267

—◆—

As a child of God, you can understand
what you need to understand.
—Mary L. Kupferle

IMAGINE THAT

There is an old adage that whatever can be perceived can be achieved. Yet I know that perception is not just a one-time thought or declaration which makes something happen; it is a thought or an image held in mind which shapes something into happening.

When I free my imagination to explore the world of possibilities, I am using a God-given ability to achieve. However, for imagination to work for me in achieving something, I must balance it with spiritual understanding that guides me along my way.

So, when my goals or plans or creative thoughts are sparked by the wisdom and love of God living out through me, I will achieve. Whatever I am able to accomplish now or in the future is never limited to what I alone can perceive—not when I infuse my hopes and dreams with spirituality.

I balance my imagination
with spiritual understanding.

DAILY WORD FOR WOMEN

Day 268

—◆—

You are not limited except
by your own thought.
—Connie Fillmore Bazzy

THINK POSITIVE My willingness to recognize and follow up with the things that help keep me healthy is essential to maintaining a healthy state of mind and body.

By thinking positive thoughts, I am developing a healthy mind. I do not let negative thoughts wear me down when I release them to God and have faith that I will be okay and that everything which concerns me will be okay.

I also eat food that I know will nourish me. A healthy heart is sustained by a healthy diet, and I eat to live a healthy life.

Friends who support me play a vital role in my healthy state of being. The company of friends brings joy and laughter into my life.

My mind and body are healthy, and I joyfully give thanks to God—the source of all life—that I am vitally alive!

I am vitally alive through God-life within me.

Day 269

—◆—

*The very least you can do in your life is
to figure out what you hope for. And the most you
can do is live inside that hope.*
—Barbara Kingsolver

CONSTANT SUPPORT At times I may yearn for less activity and confusion in my life, and yet I know that divine order is the underlying support in this and all other matters.

When I do decide to make changes in my life, I want my mind and heart to be in line with divine order. The knowledge that God is my constant source of support stimulates the confidence and courage I need. Whether my decisions are momentous or seemingly inconsequential, I am at peace.

The degree of difficulty of my journey in life may, at times, intimidate me into thinking I will stumble. Yet, because I know that the spirit of God goes before me to straighten the turns and level the rough places, I move forward with confidence.

**The spirit of God goes before me
and prepares the way.**

Day 270

—◆—

*Mistakes are lessons of wisdom. The past cannot
be changed. The future is yet in your power.*
—Mary Pickford

**GREATER
STRENGTH** An oyster can turn its irritant—a tiny
grain of sand—into a beautiful pearl. I
take a lesson from the oyster and turn
the little, everyday irritants in my life
into something of value.

I do this by forgiving myself and others. As I forgive,
I apply layers of love, understanding, and acceptance
over hurt feelings. Through forgiveness, all that would
negatively impact my health or the health of my
relationships is healed.

And if an act of forgiveness seems to call for greater
strength than I have, I call on the strength of God within
me. I give whatever forgiveness I can give—even if it is
only a little at a time. I know that out of a negative
experience, I can build a pearl.

**When I forgive, I give myself and my relationships
a chance to heal.**

CREATING A NEW LIFE
OF LOVE

BY DEE WALLACE STONE

I was away from home, shooting a movie in New Zealand, when Christopher died of a heart attack. With his passing, I lost my husband of 18 years, my daughter's father, my best friend, and my working partner. I felt as if I had lost half of all that made up my life.

It took me a day and a half to travel back home to California. I cried and grieved. I wanted more than anything to be home with our daughter, Gaby, to hold her in my arms and comfort her, but she was thousands of miles away. So I prayed for her and envisioned her surrounded by the light and love of God. I felt that the very energy of my thoughts of love were reaching out over the miles to bless her.

Fortunately, Gaby's nanny, Kristen, was with her to comfort her and to call me. The paramedics were still there when Kristen called. I asked that, as soon as the paramedics left, she let Gaby have an opportunity to say good-bye to her daddy.

Together, Gaby and Kristen said a prayer, and then Gaby told her daddy how much she loved him. She had closure with her father that I never was able to have as a child when my own father committed suicide. No one helped me say good-bye or gave me an opportunity to express my feelings. Death for me as a child was not only a great tragedy but also a haunting mystery that hung over me into adulthood.

Although she was only seven at the time, I knew that Gaby could create her life every day with her thoughts. This is true for us all: How we choose to react to something allows us to continually create and recreate our lives. We have an opportunity, always, to move on with every choice we make.

Gaby and I are still helping each other through the grieving process while moving on. A couple of years after Chris died, Gaby and I were riding home from one of her baseball games and she said, "Mommy, when are you going to start dating?"

I was taken by surprise and said, "Gaby, I don't know. Why do you ask me that?"

She looked right at me and said, "Mommy, because you need a husband, and I need a daddy." And so we started imaging and praying for the right person to come into our life, and he did. Skip and I were married last year. Gaby is very close to her new daddy. In fact, they proposed to me together. Skip took her out one New Year's Eve and told her he would like very much to be my husband and her daddy.

"What do you think about that?" he asked.

When they came home that evening, Gaby said, "Mommy, Skip and I have something very important to ask you."

I said, "Okay!"

"One, two, three," they began. Then they shouted, "Will you marry us?"

I feel so blessed. Skip is a supportive, loving husband and father.

Living from love, we help to create a life of love for ourselves and for those who share our lives. By talking and listening to God, we know there is absolutely nothing too great for God and us to handle together. We know that whenever we start a new day, a new thought, we are starting a new life. And with God, we create the very best.

Day 271

———◆———

*Don't be afraid of the space between your dreams
and reality. If you can dream it, you can make it so.*
—Belva Davis

IN-BETWEEN TIME   A change of seasons is a time when all of nature seems to be caught for a moment somewhere between what was and what will be. This in-between time is important, a time of slowing down and preparing for the months ahead.

I, too, may experience times when I need to slow down because I am not yet ready for what lies ahead. And for me this is a time of preparation, for during this time I am getting the rest I need and renewing my strength for the adventures that lie just around the corner.

God is always with me, preparing me for whatever may appear by constantly renewing my mind and my spirit. Each time I pray, I recharge the spiritual battery that enlivens my soul.

**In prayer, I am renewed. I am ready
to begin again.**

Day 272

—◆—

My mother taught me very early to believe
I could achieve any accomplishment I wanted to.
The first was to walk without braces.
—Wilma Rudolph

UNSHAKABLE FAITH   Others may tell me how they think I should live my life, and I am thankful that they care enough about me to want to be of help. However, I know that Spirit is at work in my life and that by living from the presence of God within me, I am building my life and my future on a firm foundation.

Love, harmony, peace, and joy all contribute to who I am. Grounded in these divine principles, I am unshakable. I am prepared to deal with any situation that may present itself.

Secure in the knowledge that I am guided, protected, and loved by God, I eagerly await all that life has to offer me. I am building my future firmly grounded in God's love today.

I live my life on the firm foundation
of love and faith.

Day 273

———◆———

Beloved,

Open your mind and heart to Me, and listen in blessed silence as I speak to you.

Decisions abound in your life, and you are learning to make your choices wisely by listening to Me and seeing beyond appearances to what is true. Because you believe in Me, the mysteries of My works will be revealed to you.

Having faith in Me opens a world of wonder to you. You discover that all life is sacred—in whatever form it takes. You enjoy the beauty of Earth, for it is your home. And most importantly, My beloved, you discover the beauty of each moment and the infinite possibilities that each day holds.

"What no eye has seen, nor ear heard, nor the human heart conceived, what God has prepared for those who love him."
—1 Corinthians 2:9

Day 274

—◆—

Inside myself is a place where I live all alone and
that's where you renew your springs that never dry up.
—Pearl S. Buck

SIMPLICITY How much simpler my life would be if there were no disagreements to resolve, no challenges to work out, no dilemmas to clear up!

Yet even with all of life's ups and downs, I can enjoy stress-free simplicity by allowing God's gentle spirit to work in and through me.

In prayer, gently—oh, so gently—God takes me by the hand and leads me into a realization of peace and contentment. Here with God, I am open to the wonders of life.

Here with God, I understand that the most complex situation becomes simple. I gain a new perspective, a clarity of purpose that gives me the strength I need to live life fully—every moment of the day.

God's gentle spirit brings clarity to my life.

DAILY WORD FOR WOMEN

Day 275

—◆—

Life is what we make it,
always has been, always will be.
—Grandma Moses

THE REAL ME

Through experience, I know that the cover of a book may not always be a good indicator that a story of quality and inspiration is within. And the same is true of people. How can a first impression based on a person's looks ever be a true representation of the real person?

I know that the real me—the life of God that is within—is pure of heart and mind. The real me is centered in God, and the truth about me is that I am an expression of divine love and life. These qualities—along with peace, understanding, and comfort—are my divine inheritance.

Beneath my changing outer appearance, my inner being remains the same. In the sacred sanctuary of my soul, I am totally one with God.

I am an expression of divine love and life.

Day 276

*The best and most beautiful things in the world
cannot be seen, nor touched . . . but are felt in the heart.*
—Helen Keller

**WINGS
OF
SPIRIT**

The freedom to be all that I long to be lies within me. God's spirit sets me free! On the wings of His spirit I soar to new heights of spiritual understanding. I can never again be captive to any negativity or limitation.

The spirit of God has set me free, and I express that freedom by being all I was created to be: I am intelligent, I am strong, I am happy—I am free! I can remain free because I accept my freedom without hesitation or worry, without limitation or doubt.

The possibilities for me are endless, and I prepare myself for those possibilities by releasing anything from my mind or heart that does not contain the truth of spiritual freedom. I think thoughts that promote my own freedom and the freedom of everyone.

The spirit of God has set me free!

Day 277

◆

*Joy is the feeling
of grinning inside.*
—*Melba Colgrove*

LAUGHTER God, when I laugh, I feel renewed and revitalized. Until I laugh, I may not realize how tense I have become. Then—over something that may be amusing only to me—I laugh. And with that laugh, the door to my soul opens a crack, allowing inner joy to rush out and push aside thoughts about any problems.

Feeling no stress—even for a moment—I am able to relax. After letting the joy of Your spirit within shine out from me, I think more clearly. It is amazing, but the laughter I release seems to nourish me as much as any food or water I could take in.

I want laughter in my life every day, and God, I know it will be when I let the joy of Your presence within be expressed as gladness in my life and about all life.

**Through laughter, I express
the inner joy of spirit.**

Day 278

—◆—

Everyone has an invisible sign hanging from their neck saying, "Make me feel important." Never forget this message when working with people.
—*Mary Kaye Ashe*

DIVERSITY Some children label other children and adults with names based on physical or mental attributes that seem different from their own. Hopefully, these children will learn that everyone is worthy of respect, that diversity presents some incredibly interesting friends and associations.

And it is true. I, myself, help create a world of harmony by recognizing that the only true label for any person is this: a divine expression of harmony in action.

I honor and respect the diversity of those around me, understanding that harmony is a way of life and an attitude that I can carry with me and freely share with others. Then I live my life as a divine expression of harmony in action!

I am divine harmony in action!

Day 279

---◆---

*Failure: Is it a limitation? Bad timing? It's a lot of things.
It is something you cannot be afraid of, because you
will stop growing. The next step beyond failure could be
your biggest success in life.—Debbie Allen*

FAITH BOOSTER If ever I doubt my own ability or whenever I feel uncertain about anything in life, God gently reminds me that I need not be frightened, for I cannot travel beyond the reach of divine love.

And what a faith booster that is for me! How reassuring it is to know that I am always in the midst of God's loving presence. So even if I sometimes feel that I just cannot go on, that I just don't have the energy to complete some task, I remember my faith and focus on God, not outer appearances.

God is all-power—power that moves any mountain of a challenge out of my way and even out of my life. With God, there is nothing I cannot do. So I place my wholehearted faith in God and watch the miracles happen!

Divine love is always with me.

Day 280

—◆—

Beloved,

Within the rich fields of your soul, I have sown the seeds of your divine potential. Love will nourish these seeds, and faith will sustain them.

You are My creation, and My spirit is within you. Your eyes twinkle with the joy of My presence. Your actions convey self-confidence and creativity.

Experience is your teacher, My beloved. Take what you discover each day and build upon it— relying on the wisdom you receive from Me. I will satisfy your thirst for knowledge, for I am the answer to all your needs.

"O God, you are my God, I seek you,
my soul thirsts for you."
—Psalm 63:1

Day 281

—◆—

Perfect trust in God is the secret
of perfect relaxation, rest, and renewal.
—Clara Palmer

Sometimes it seems that the harder I try to accomplish something, the more difficult it becomes. Then, when I relax and allow God to guide me, whatever I am doing becomes easier. The project itself did not change, but my attitude about it did when I included God in my plans.

I have a purpose to fulfill in life—a divine purpose. I may not know the exact details of all that is included in this purpose, but God knows. And God will be with me to guide my way and strengthen my resolve.

The knowledge of my divine connection in everyday living empowers me to take great strides forward. I am filled with confidence. And because I know that God and I are capable of great things, I enjoy the challenges as well as the achievements in life.

I relax and know that God is my guide
to all my achievements.

Day 282

The cure for all the ills and wrongs, the cares, the sorrows,
and the crimes of humanity, all lie in that one word "love."
It is the divine vitality that everywhere produces and
restores life.—Lydia Maria Child

ABUNDANCE I know and feel God's loving presence within me. When I look around me, I see the evidence of God's love everywhere. God has provided everything I could ever need to find fulfillment in a nurturing environment.

Out of the abundance of God's love, I receive. I gratefully accept the blessings God has for me, because I know that whatever blesses me, I can somehow share with others.

God never ceases to bless me! Longtime friends, loving relationships, physical strength, emotional well-being—all are blessings that I give heartfelt thanks for every day. Above all else, however, I am thankful for God—a loving Creator who gives attention to me.

Out of an abundance of love, God blesses me.

Day 283

—◆—

The silence is a kind of stillness,
a place of retreat into which we may enter
and having entered, may know the Truth.
—Myrtle Fillmore

SACRED SPACE

There is no better time than now, no better place than right where I am to immerse myself in God's presence in me and the holy presence all around me.

God is everywhere, so the very ground on which I stand is holy ground, a sacred space where God and I are one. In this sacred space, I am free from any limitation, free from anything that would hold me back or keep me from expressing God's love.

As I become more in tune with God's presence everywhere, I also become more aware of God's presence within others. The presence of God is a beacon of love that draws me to others and allows us to live together in peace.

In this sacred space, we are one with God and one with each other.

God is with me in this sacred space.

Day 284

♦

For many, the power of God's love keeps drawing them.
Like a wildflower in a thicket, the original message
of encompassing love continues to poke its head through
the briars, beckoning. People yearn to feel that power.
—Adele Wilcox

OUTPOURING OF LOVE I am a living, breathing miracle in action every time I let go and let God be God in me and in my life. I gratefully accept every blessing as an outpouring of love and caring from a loving, caring Creator.

As I cease to worry and allow the spirit of God to move out through my words and actions, I see that the results are miraculous. Where before I may have felt confusion and saw no choice that seemed workable, I now see that there is a way—a clear way.

The cloud of doubt has lifted and been scattered by the powerful activity of divine understanding. I appreciate that life itself is a miracle, for it is a divine plan of the Creator.

I am blessed every time I let go and let God
be God in me and in my life.

Day 285

— ◆ —

We are never alone when we try to do the right thing.
God is always with us, making us a majority.
—Mary Katherine MacDougall

NEVER ALONE At some phase in my life—whether I have moved out on my own, ended a relationship, or lost a loved one—I may be living alone for the first time. But in this and all other circumstances, my faith in God will sustain me.

I can never really be alone because God's presence is with me to guide me in all that I do. God provides for my needs—the comfort I seek, the assurance I desire. And if I do find myself without human companionship, I use that time of solitude to become more aware of God.

In the presence of God, I am given unconditional love and acceptance. The indwelling spirit of God is the source of life which energizes me and the breath of life which renews me. God has given me life, and through the life I live, I bless others. No, I am never alone, for God is with me now and always.

In the presence of God, I receive unconditional love and acceptance.

Day 286

—◆—

God does not ask your ability or your inability.
He asks only your availability.
—Mary Kaye Ashe

AWARE OF GOD

Being in my right place may mean I am not always comfortable with everything that is happening in my life. Working through problems and gaining understanding, I sometimes stretch beyond what I believe I can do. But, thank God, I discover I can do more.

Whether I am starting a new job or a new relationship, I have much to learn and to share. Whether I am continuing on a familiar path or blazing a new trail, there is something for me to give and receive.

And there is really no mystery to unravel; I know that I can always be in my right place. I will be when I know that any place is right as long as I am totally aware of God's presence.

God is with me now—in this very place.

Day 287

—◆—

Beloved,

When you said yes to living your life as the divine creation you are, you opened yourself fully to My presence. Then a surge of My love for you sparked your creativity. How fully you felt your connection with My wisdom and guidance.

Never questioning why, you did your best wherever you were and in whatever was yours to do. All the while, you knew that I was with you. I observed as looks of doubt lifted from your eyes and you committed yourself to a divine mission.

It is true: I am always aware of you, so remember always to be aware of Me and My love for you.

"Your hands have made and fashioned me; give me understanding that I may learn your commandments."
—Psalm 119:73

Day 288

———◆———

Spiritual growth is something you can only feel for yourself. No number of words ever written can take the place of your own personal, mystical experiences which occur on the path to spiritual growth.—Rebecca Clark

GENTLE GUIDE

Loving Spirit, thank You for filling me with Your light and constantly showing me the way. You gently guide me so that I am sure and steady. You lead me in doing what is most helpful for everyone concerned, and You remind me to be confident and stand firm as I do.

You direct my thoughts so that I am enriched by divine ideas. And You help me use those ideas to enhance the lives of those around me.

Loving Spirit, here are my hands, my heart, my whole being. I want to be Your light and love in action. I am ready to spread goodwill wherever I am. In all I do, I trust in Your unfailing light, which radiates out from me to embrace others with wisdom and understanding.

I am guided by the loving spirit of God.

Day 289

*We need to stir up that creative imagination
and expand horizons; having a positive outlook
helps us stay healthy.*
—Ardath Rodale

HEART BLESSING   Each beat of my heart is a blessing, for each beat ensures that the oxygen I need is circulating to all the cells of my body. What a miraculous organ my heart is!

Yet my heart is so much more than an organ that pumps blood throughout my body. It is also a spiritual center within me, circulating divine love into every part and particle of my being.

And like each heartbeat, each loving thought I think is a blessing that nourishes me. Loving thought after thought is generated from my heart center.

In wave after wave, the constant assurance of God's love is in perfect rhythm with the steady beat of my heart.

**With all my heart, I give thanks to God
for creating me to express love.**

Day 290

$\blacklozenge$

Forgiveness is a unification of the soul with God,
comparable to the raindrop's reception by the sea.
—Imelda Shanklin

I CAN
FORGIVE

Who is the only one who can limit my capacity to forgive? Me! Yet why should I? Through unlimited forgiveness, I release the burden of former hurts and begin again.

This willingness to forgive takes some practice, but I can do it. I can forgive. If there is anything I have done that I regret, I forgive myself and let it go. I am not acting irresponsibly, because as I release, I make a commitment to do better in the future.

And if there is anything that anyone has done which caused me sorrow or pain, I forgive them. As I release all hurtful memories about them, I feel a healing happening within me.

From the love of God in my own heart,
I forgive myself and others.

Day 291

*The way to increased faith, belief, and receptivity
is through prayer. Prayer opens us up to receive
the life that's always there.*
—Connie Fillmore Bazzy

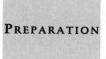

PREPARATION

Being prepared is generally a good rule of thumb to consider when undertaking a new project. Planning ahead and considering all options make it easier for me once the project is under way.

And the best way that I can plan ahead for any project—whether it is personal or business-related—is to pray about it. God is and always will be my first and most valued counselor. I can trust that the guidance I receive will be the firm foundation on which I base my decisions.

When I am prepared, I meet any challenge with faith, which allows me to clear my thoughts and focus on the task at hand. All my projects and plans begin with God's loving guidance.

Yes, it is true:
With God, I am prepared.

Day 292

◆

No matter what happens, keep on beginning and failing. Each time you fail, start all over again, and you will grow stronger until you find that you have accomplished a purpose—not the one you began with perhaps, but one you will be glad to remember.—Anne Sullivan

COMPLETION

As the new day dawns, I am given a brand-new opportunity to begin again, to start fresh in both new and familiar matters. Yet as sunset draws near, I realize that endings are just as important. Without the sunset, I cannot witness the magnificence of a new sunrise as it paints its vibrant hues across the morning sky.

And just as morning turns into day and day into night, each new beginning inevitably leads me to a time when I can savor a feeling of completion. How comforting to know that every ending will lead me to a new beginning! Like the darkness before the dawn, my darkest hours will always give way to the promise of a new morning.

Every ending leads to a new beginning.

Day 293

—◆—

I learned in my four decades in Washington
that one person can make a difference.
—Liz Carpenter

SPIRITUAL UNDER-STANDING In order to live in harmony with others, I do not necessarily have to agree with them on all or even most things.

Harmony is the calm of one person that allows others the freedom to express their own ideas. It is a reverence that embraces the differences of people as a sacred plan of God's design.

So whether I am expressing harmony as a loving parent or guiding other youngsters into adulthood, I rely on spiritual understanding to direct me. I do not force anyone to fit into some preconceived mold.

Harmony thrives in an atmosphere of spiritual understanding. My willingness to recognize both my own sacredness and the sacredness of all people gives birth to a peace that passes both understanding and misunderstanding.

I live and work in harmony with others.

Day 294

—◆—

Beloved,

Every moment of your life has led you to where you are right now, for every moment is a time of spiritual preparation that guides you and helps you to express the infinite potential within you.

Listen to your heart. Can you hear the sweet echoes of My love for you? Accept My love and let it be the basis for all your actions as it flows out from you to others.

Let go of the past, let go of worries, and forgive what you can. I will do the rest. You are My beloved, and I am even now preparing the way for blessing upon blessing to come into your life.

Are you ready for a blessing? With the understanding you have gained so far, you are discovering that you truly are ready, that you are prepared in mind and heart to realize your dreams.

"In all your ways acknowledge him,
and he will make straight your paths."
—Proverbs 3:6

Day 295

◆

It is not easy to find happiness in ourselves,
and it is not possible to find it elsewhere.
—*Agnes Repplier*

GOD-POWER

If I have ever tried to rev up my willpower in order to start or stop doing something, I have probably learned that there are times when it seems like the more I try, the more difficult it becomes.

Although I may be willing to give up on myself, I know that God will never give up on me. So I call on God-power. When I am trying to control my habits or any of my behaviors, I am saying that they have the power to control me. The truth is that God is the one power, and with God moving through me as the power to stop something negative or start something positive, I will be successful.

I am more than equal to whatever it is I desire to accomplish. I am because God is the power that not only sparks my will but also constantly recharges it.

God is the supreme power that sparks
my will to be successful.

Day 296

— ◆ —

He who laughs, lasts.
—Mary Pettibone Poole

**J O Y
IN MY
S O U L**

God, Your spirit within me is the source of every gladness I have ever experienced or could ever experience. The moment I accepted Your presence as the joy in my soul, I awakened to a delight of spirit that words cannot describe.

Joy in my soul comforts me in my times alone—whether I am living alone for the first time or have been for many years. I may not always feel included in a circle of friends or family, but I know that You always encircle me with love and caring. I need never face anything alone.

Joy in my soul heals me. The gladness of Your spirit living through me cleanses me of any condition that would work against my health and vitality. God, You are the gladness of my whole being, and I am at peace and totally well.

God, You are the joy in my soul.

Day 297

◆

No artist is ahead of his time.
He is the time.
—*Martha Graham*

IN THE NOW   When something happens that affects me deeply, it is easy for me to become so involved in such an event that everything else fades away. I live completely in the moment and do not allow anything to distract me from what I am seeing or feeling or doing.

Yet at times I may forget to stay focused. Then I become distracted and forget to live every moment as if it were the most important moment of my life. I can change this! I can make the choice to live each moment to the fullest by not worrying about things from the past or about what may happen in the future.

The past is over and the future will take care of itself. Right now, this present moment, is where I am. Every minute spent in full awareness is a sacred time in which I can become more aware of God's loving presence within me and around me.

Each moment that I am totally aware
of God is a sacred time.

Day 298

—◆—

Life's under no obligation to give us
what we expect.
—Margaret Mitchell

WORKING WITH GOD

How do I help people who are going through a challenge to find strength and comfort?

Do I say anything to them other than to offer an encouraging word? Perhaps the answer lies in my own faith in God—faith that God is guiding them and that the right outcome is even now coming about.

Whether I am conscious of it or not, God's will is actively at work in my life and in the lives of others. And as we each recognize this truth and work with God rather than worrying about the next step, we will find that our lives are so much smoother.

So I know for myself and others that we are beings of eternal oneness and strength. God offers each of us comfort and support, and because God is always supporting us, each day is brighter than the day before.

I let God's will be my will.

Day 299

---◆---

The purpose of life is growth. This growth always
is toward God. There can be no growth without freedom.
—Stella Terrill Mann

**TAKE
A GOOD
LOOK**
When I first look at a painting, I see color, form, and texture, but when I take time to study the painting, I discover so much detail and artistry. And the same is true when I take a good look at myself. So I take time to study the details of my life and determine whether the things I regularly do—my habits—are in my best interests.

Even negative habits can be comforting—but that comfort is temporary. The long-term effects of negative habits can be harmful. Yet with faith in God and God in me, I can shake off unwanted habits.

As I begin anew, I no longer feel vulnerable or the need to hide behind habits. I am free! Spirit is protecting, loving, and guiding me through the day and making my way easier.

**Through the power of Spirit
within, I am free.**

Day 300

—◆—

Sometimes a life, like a house, needs renovating—the smell of new wood, new rooms in the heart, unimagined until one begins the work. One rebuilds because the structure deserves a renewing.—Doris Schwerin

KEY TO HEALING

What is the key that unlocks the flow of healing life within me? Faith is an important key, a tool that I use to uncover new understanding.

It is the very spirit of God that enlivens and renews me. My understanding faith sparks a current of life and healing that surges throughout my body.

There is no turning back; I am moving forward with new life in a new life. At first I may only notice a slight improvement. I may move about more easily and even think more clearly. Yet the fact that I am refreshed is unmistakable.

The spirit of God is the life and vitality that fills me and thrills me. I am alive with the life of God!

I am alive with the life of God!

A GLIMPSE OF THE ETERNAL
BY JOAN LAUREN

Just a few weeks after we were engaged, Ken was diagnosed with cancer. One day in the hospital, Ken was in so much pain that I couldn't bear to watch. As I walked out of his room, I saw a woman pushing a cradle down the hall.

The woman didn't say a word, but she looked at me with such warmth in her eyes that I was drawn to her and the cradle. However, as I looked down at the thin, pale child, I thought I was going to scream.

Then, suddenly, the child smiled at me—and that smile penetrated deep inside me and awakened me to a truth I desperately needed to know—for her, for me, and for Ken. She was telling me, "My body is like this, but Spirit is alive in me, and I am joyous."

I understood that although the body is temporary, Spirit within is eternal. Her smile gave me a glimpse of the eternal life that is in us all.

Day 301

—◆—

Beloved,

You are My joy, My love, My life. And you are expressing these qualities in your life as you work with Me to bring a greater spiritual awareness to those whose lives you touch.

So let My love and joy be in your conversations, your activities, and your thoughts. As you hold firm to your beliefs, look around you. Can you see what a magnificent blessing you are?

As your faith grows stronger and stronger with each passing day, it is becoming the key to your success in every endeavor—in healing yourself and in helping to heal your community.

Thank you, beloved, for your dedication to living from the love and life that I have placed within you.

"God is able to provide you with every blessing in abundance, so that . . . you may share abundantly in every good work."
—2 Corinthians 9:8

Day 302

— ◆ —

In search of my mother's garden,
I found my own.
—Alice Walker

REVERENCE When I look at the vastness of an ocean or stand at the foot of a towering mountain, I am awestruck by the power and glory of God. And I feel especially filled with reverence when I realize that the divine energy which created such majesty also created me.

As I consider the beauty and greatness of natural wonders, I might feel insignificant in comparison. However, I know nothing could be further from the truth. I am not insignificant at all! I am important and unique, for I, too, am God's creation.

This understanding fills me with a deep sense of peace that lingers like the pleasing aroma of a flowering garden. As I live each day from the peace and strength within me, I remember who I am: a creation of the Almighty.

I am at peace, for I am one of God's beloved creations.

Day 303

—◆—

No one can make you feel inferior
without your consent.
—Eleanor Roosevelt

BRING OUT THE BEST

When I follow through on a commitment to enhance my physical, emotional, and spiritual well-being by letting go and letting God, I am doing something to bring out the best in me and through me.

I clear my mind of all concerns, stress, and confusion that would come between me and the desires of my heart. I am doing something important each time I consciously invite God to bring about something that magnifies the presence of the Divine in me and in my life.

It is as if I am saying, "Here I am, God, a supple piece of clay that You can mold into something magnificent. Your spirit shapes me day by day, revealing that what I thought was a flaw only needed the divine touch in order to be recognized as beauty and strength that were waiting to be revealed."

Here I am, God, ready for You to reveal
spiritual strength through me.

Day 304

—◆—

If we had no winter, the spring would not be
so pleasant. If we did not sometimes taste of adversity,
prosperity would not be so welcome.
—Anne Bradstreet

A NEW DAWN Every day is a divine-order day that begins with the sun rising over the horizon into the breaking of a new dawn. Nature follows a pattern of divine order, and I follow nature's example by allowing God to guide my every action.

Today is a divine-order day! I did not cause the sun to shine—only God can do that. But my faith in God will never cease and assures me the sun will rise each day. Even if clouds block my view, I know the sun is there—just temporarily beyond sight but waiting to shine on me.

Today is a divine-order day! Rather than taking life for granted, I celebrate the wonder of it and welcome each new day. I thank God that today and every day is a divine-order day!

I celebrate the wonder of this day!

Day 305

—◆—

One of the things I learned the hard way was that it doesn't pay to get discouraged. Keeping busy and making optimism a way of life can restore your faith.
—Lucille Ball

LANGUAGE OF FAITH

My love for God transcends words, but I know that God always listens and hears the language of my heart— a language of faith and gratitude.

I trust in divine wisdom and follow the guidance that God pours out to me. My faith shows forth as love, joy, and self-confidence.

I pray that my loved ones will always feel the peace which comes from knowing God's presence in their lives. From this sacred experience, they will feel the same joy of living that I feel right now.

God provides everything—from the essentials, such as the air I breathe and the food I eat, to added blessings, such as good friends and a safe, secure home.

Spirit divine, I have faith in You.

Day 306

—◆—

What makes humility so desirable is the marvelous thing it does to us; it creates in us a capacity for the closest possible intimacy with God.
—Monica Baldwin

TRUE PICTURE

One challenge in an otherwise perfect day can seem to overshadow my whole day—but only if I let it. So I concentrate on holding a true picture of myself in mind. And the truest picture of me is always one in which I am vitalized, strengthened, and guided by the very spirit of God.

During times when I am asked to do more than I may believe I can do, I bring to mind my true picture. And this is who I see: a calm and powerful, loving and compassionate being infused by Spirit. Then a new resolve and a new energy rise up from the depths of my being.

I carry a true picture of my loved ones in my mind and heart. With every thought, word, and act, I encourage the fulfillment of our spiritual reality.

**I hold my spiritual identity in mind—
a true picture of me.**

Day 307

—◆—

Were there no God, we would be in this glorious world
with grateful hearts and no one to thank.
—Christina Rossetti

GOD BLESSES ME

God, You are the source of my life, of all life, and I give thanks that Your love for me has no limits or bounds.

Every time I look around, I appreciate Your abundance and a multitude of my blessings become evident to me. No matter where I go, I am always surrounded by Your presence.

You bless me with love—love that fills me and flows out from me to others through a gentle smile, a kind gesture, a friendly word of encouragement.

You bless me with hope—hope that is made even stronger by my faith in Your unfailing presence. In all that I do, God, I am prosperous, and I give thanks to You.

God showers me with blessing upon blessing.

Day 308

———— ◆ ————

Beloved,

As the sunlight warms your face, feel the glow of My love caressing you. Carry that feeling of warmth with you in all that you do. Feel My presence strengthening you as you go about doing your best. With Me to guide you, you cannot fail, for all your actions will be learning experiences.

Each tomorrow will be a new dawn in which you continue to bring out the best in yourself and in others. Your faith will guide you to succeed. As others see your faith in action, they will learn from you and follow your example.

The blessings of the future are yours, for you are My beloved creation. Never will there be a time when I am not with you—loving you, blessing you, guiding you into the new dawn of opportunities that await you.

"By the tender mercy of our God, the dawn from on high will break upon us."
—Luke 1:78

Day 309

— ◆ —

*The real art of conversation is not only to say
the right thing in the right place, but to leave unsaid
the wrong thing at the tempting moment.*
—Dorothy Nevill

**NEW
PURPOSE**

At times I may be critical of myself,
asking, "Why did I do that?" or "Why
didn't I do this?" The saving grace for
me is the unconditional love of God—
divine grace that transforms the dark of night into the
brightness of dawn, the despair of doubt into the joy
of hope.

In the grace of God, I discover a new purpose in
living. I settle for nothing less than a life lived in the love
and acceptance of the Creator.

I have patience with myself—a patience that allows
divine ideas to take root and come to full maturity in
me. And what I accept for myself, I can and do accept
for others. Knowing that the grace of God is a blessing
for all, I extend my love, patience, and acceptance to
everyone.

Divine grace transforms me and my life.

Day 310

◆

The future belongs to those who believe
in the beauty of their dreams.
—Eleanor Roosevelt

EACH STEP — Every journey begins with a single step, and if I am beginning my spiritual journey toward a greater knowledge of God, I take that step with confidence and certainty.

I use each moment as a stepping-stone to more awareness of my spiritual nature. Step by step, I become increasingly more in tune with Spirit and allow divine power to express itself through me as wisdom. I discover that when I use spiritual vision, I see wonderful possibilities which are available to me as part of my divine inheritance.

This spiritual journey of mine will encompass a lifetime of ever-increasing awareness. And I do not worry as I move along, because I know that God is in charge and gently holds my hand.

I am on a journey of spiritual discovery.

Day 311

◆

I am a little pencil in the hand of a writing God who
is sending a love letter to the world.
—*Mother Teresa*

HIGH CALLING
What higher calling could anyone have than to love and accept people with the compassion and understanding of the Creator of all life?

And so I answer the call to be loving, to recognize my family, friends, and co-workers as magnificent works of the Master Creator. When my response is from the love of God within, I am blessed and I bless others. Love rushes in to soothe any pain, to mend any rifts, to smooth out any rough spots in our relationships.

Acceptance of others grows from the love of God within. Therefore, I do not make the mistake of trying to change others into what I think they should be. Acceptance of the diversity of people is also an acceptance of God as the supreme guide and source of life for each person.

Master Creator, I love and I accept
Your magnificent works.

Day 312

—◆—

Life is not the way it is supposed to be. It is the way it is.
The way you cope with it is what makes the difference.
—Virginia Satir

LIFE God is spirit, and the spirit of God surges through me in a healing flow that cleanses, strengthens, and renews me. I am healthy and whole!

The life of God within me is the same life that enlivens the whole universe. I am amazed when I think about the power available to me through a spiritual connection with God. Yet it is available to me—any time I need it, any time I need to renew my mind, body, or emotions.

I am alive! I am whole! I am one with the healing life of God! Because I am one with God's healing life, I am one with a source of energy that charges me with energy and reactivates my enthusiasm for living. I am ready and willing to move forward in the glorious adventure called life!

The life of God surges through me, healing me
and making me strong.

Day 313

◆

There is hope if people will begin to awaken that spiritual part of themselves—that heartfelt acknowledgement that we are the caretakers of life on this planet.
—Brooke Medicine Eagle

THANKS-GIVING

There are not enough hours in the day to thank God for all my blessings, for God is continually blessing me. So I say, "Thank You, God, for life and for all the blessings in my life. You have given me a sacred trust, and I do not take that responsibility lightly."

I show my appreciation for God's greatness as well as speaking it. When I am interacting with others or enjoying the great outdoors, I treat everyone and everything with love and respect. I honor the wonder that God has created.

I also express my thanksgiving by sharing the blessings I have already received. I devote time and energy to helping others. Just maybe my best way of thanking God is living my life in appreciation of God.

Through God's blessings, I am fulfilled.

Day 314

—◆—

All of us, no matter what our place in life, no matter what we do, whether we realize it or not, are serving God.
—Martha Smock

RECOGNITION Behind every great work, deed, or action, there are usually some unsung heroes who have helped. And while I may not always receive recognition from others, I know that God recognizes my contributions. Above all else, God knows.

God recognizes even my intention to bless. By dedicating myself and what I do to God, I am naturally blessed with a return of the faith and love—from many people and in diverse circumstances.

And throughout the day, I remind myself to recognize others who help me. I give thanks for the people who provide the clean environment in which I work and the person who delivers the mail to my home. I give thanks for everyone who has touched my life in some way.

The God-life in me recognizes
the God-life in all others.

Day 315

---◆---

Beloved,

You will know many people throughout your life. Some will be a part of your circle of family and friends for a lifetime, others for just a short time. However long they are with you, each of these people has the capacity to bless you.

Recognize the blessings that they are by looking beyond appearances to the roles these people have played in your life story. Some will be examples for you to learn by, while others will serve as companions.

I have created a vast and diverse world, and all of My creations serve a purpose—just as you do. You are all in this time and this place for a reason—because I love and care for each and every one of you.

"It is the spirit that gives life. . . .
The words that I have spoken to you
are spirit and life."
—John 6:63

Day 316

♦

Learn appreciation. Be willing to take lovingly each small gift of life, receive it, acknowledge that you have received it, appreciate it. . . . You won't be happy with more until you're happy with what you've got.—Viki King

TODAY! I can imagine myself doing so much more if only I could create more time in my day. A couple of added hours to do the things I plan to do when I have time would turn my life around.

Yet the reality is that God gives me the same number of hours in each day as every other person in the world is given. What I do with my time is up to me. Out of each day I have the freedom to create my own life. Because I realize this, I feel in control and not limited by time. It is as if God is saying to me, "Here is a fresh 24-hour day for you to do with what you will."

Then whatever I do, I do with enthusiasm, contributing and receiving something of meaning and worth.

God, thank You for this day—a time of fulfillment and meaning.

Day 317

— ◆ —

Laughter can be more satisfying than honor,
more precious than money.
—Harriet Rochlin

FOUNTAIN OF JOY Children just naturally seem to know how to express the joy of spirit: They laugh and play and sing and dance whenever they feel the urge. And as they express their delight, they are wonderful examples of how it is to be happy and enthusiastic about life.

Laughter and play are every bit as important to my sense of well-being as good nutrition and exercise are. And recognizing the fountain of joy that is within me is the first step in letting my own joy come out.

What wonder and excitement I feel when I let joy be a natural part of my everyday life. And what benefits I reap when I give myself permission to laugh and to play.

Then I am relaxed and so much more aware of God, because I am taking time to truly enjoy the beauty and wonder of God's world.

Yes, it's true: The spirit of God is a wellspring of joy within me!

Day 318

*When we help others to greater and greater freedom
in living, we are helping ourself to greater living.*
—*Stella Terrill Mann*

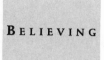

BELIEVING   Wanting to do well may motivate me temporarily, but believing I can do well gives me the constant assurance I need in order to excel.

And I have learned that it is not so much my wanting freedom as it is my believing I can have it that sets my mind at ease and allows me to be creative and confident. However, such a belief is based on the power and presence of God in me, rather than on my past performances or current circumstances. Believing in God in me frees me to express inner strength and wisdom.

I have both freedom from negative habits and the freedom to express what fulfills me. As I let God in me come through in everyday living, I am free to be my very best.

The spirit of God within me is my source of freedom.

Day 319

—◆—

When any of us get to the point where we feel as if there's no hope and we don't know what direction to take or what's going to work, it's words like "let go and let God" that will pop up as if they were sent by God to get us through.—Rolonda Watts

TURN AROUND

Letting go of a troubling thought about what could or might happen can be a challenge. Perhaps I am giving so much attention to the problem that I cannot possibly see that there is a solution. However, there is a way to turn from fear and anxiety to faith and peace of mind: I turn from thinking about the trouble to thinking about God.

And what I do after I release a problem is critical to my not taking it back or creating a bigger one: I give it to God for a solution. As I turn any problem over to God, I also turn my life around. I open my mind and my life to divine solutions, knowing that they come about through the love, order, and peace of God that is available to me always.

I turn my life around by turning to the light of God.

Day 320

—◆—

*Our soul longs for God. All of our desires represent
the deep longing of our soul for oneness with God.*
—Rebecca Clark

REFRESHING BREAK If I allow myself to become caught up in the activities of the day, I may find I am so busy that I forget to take time to pray. Yet when I do take a moment to retreat from the outer world for a heart-and-soul connection with God, I immediately feel refreshed. I am comforted and strengthened.

In prayer, I quiet my thoughts. I let my body relax and allow God's loving presence to support me.

Prayer is my comfort, for it satisfies my yearning for God. I understand that my prayers do not cause God to act; instead, they help me realize that God's will is actively at work, bringing about blessings for me at all times.

**Prayer is the refreshing break that brings me comfort
and peace of mind.**

Day 321

—◆—

*The love between husband and wife, between parents
and children, is just the least little bit of God, as pushed
forth through visible form into manifestation.*
—H. Emilie Cady

**PRAYER
FOR
LOVED
ONES**

As I think about my family and
friends, I feel so very grateful for them.
They have given me love and
acceptance, and I want to bless them
in return. So I take this opportunity to give thanks for
them and to remember them in my prayers:

"God, from the depths of Your love in my heart, I
give thanks for my loved ones. They are Your unique
creations, and I thank You for the privilege of loving
them and being loved by them. Wherever they go this
day, my loving thoughts go with them.

"God, Your spirit glows within my loved ones and
lights their way. They are Your beloved, and I give
thanks that they live in the shelter of Your presence."

**The spirit of God glows brightly within my loved ones,
lighting their way.**

Day 322

---◆---

Beloved,

Yes, it is true: I give you a fresh 24 hours each day. You take that time and create something of meaning in order to fulfill a divine purpose in the way you live your life.

Your joy in giving expression to life fills the atmosphere around you with beauty. Believing that you can achieve great accomplishments, you do. And all the while, I am with you to help you over any rough spots you may encounter.

You are refreshed by spending time with Me in prayer, by consciously knowing that I will accept whatever you give to Me and offer a divine solution.

Know that as much as you love and appreciate others, they love and appreciate you. You bring the freshness of spring to every day, to every experience, and to everyone you meet.

"When I thought, 'My foot is slipping,'
your steadfast love, O Lord, held me up."
—Psalm 94:18

Day 323

———◆———

Remember, the greatest gift is not found in a store nor under a tree, but in the hearts of true friends.
—Cindy Lew

INTERACTING IN HARMONY

Whenever the subject of harmony comes up, I think of my own friendships and relationships. I think about how committed I am to including harmony and goodwill in my interactions with others. Yet before I can contribute harmony to any environment, I need to feel harmony within myself.

And I do when I am fulfilled by the way I live my life and by the thoughts that I think. Such satisfaction comes as I let the love of God think and live through me.

God's love is the foundation upon which I build my life, so I cannot help but be in harmony with who I am and what I am about. My decisions are founded on divine love, so I am confident that my actions and thoughts will be loving and harmonious.

**I am committed to expressing harmony
and goodwill in my relationships.**

Day 324

——◆——

*The silence is not something mysterious. It is
that inner place of stillness where you feel
and know your oneness with God.*
—*May Rowland*

**SILENTLY
I PRAY**
When I become quiet and focused
on the spirit of God within me, I feel a
resurgence of energy. By turning
within, I rechannel the energy that I
would have exerted toward outer conditions and
circumstances.

Alone with the presence of God, I am serene. I
rediscover how refreshing it feels to be calm and at
peace with my own thoughts. Lingering in the silence, I
feel as if waves of peace are washing over me and
clearing away any tenseness and anxiety.

I do not need to speak aloud. My silent prayer is a
message of truth that vibrates in every fiber of my
being: "O God, You are my God. You satisfy the thirst
of my soul for comfort and love."

**In the silence of prayer, I understand
that I am eternally one with God.**

Day 325

—◆—

There is nothing to fear, for you are always
and forever in the presence of God.
—Martha Smock

DIVINE GRACE

If someone were to ask me what I considered God's grace to be, my answer would come without hesitation: God's grace is the assurance that I am always in the presence of God and one with the eternal love of God.

Grace is the beauty and blessing of each new day—a day to live in oneness with my Creator. Every opportunity before me is a direct result of grace.

The love and appreciation I feel for God fill me and flow from me to others through the things I say and the actions I take. I know that God gently guides me in the way I am to go, and I make the choice to listen to and follow such divine wisdom.

Grace is the assurance of God's presence within me and God's love for me.

Day 326

♦

God, I can push the grass apart
And lay my finger on Thy heart!
—Edna St. Vincent Millay

IMAGINATION Changing a blank canvas into a masterpiece or a block of stone into a priceless sculpture takes imagination and creativity. Yet the people who have produced such treasures had to move beyond imagining in order to do so. They took the necessary steps to make what they had imagined become a reality.

Imagination opens the door to divinely inspired ideas and awakens me to unlimited possibilities. So as I envision harmony in my life, I begin to take the necessary steps toward realizing that dream.

As I imagine people helping each other, I see the value of teamwork in times of need and the satisfaction received when one creation of God helps another. What a blessing it is to know that whatever can be envisioned is a possibility!

My imagination opens the door
to unlimited possibilities.

Day 327

— ◆ —

Love is the oxygen of spiritual growth, and spiritual growth is the basis of physical health.
—*Mary-Alice Jafolla*

RESTORATION

I want to experience life as the amazing creation of God that I was created to be. So I remember that my body is a home for the Creator of life. The wonder of God created me and is constantly healing me. I can bless my mind and body each day in life-affirming prayer:

"Spirit of life, I release any thought of concern and invite the blessing of Your healing love into my thoughts and my life.

"Beloved Spirit, bless my arms and legs and keep them strong and healthy. And bless my heart for the powerful work that it does. Your healing love flows throughout my body, keeping me vibrant and alive.

"Mighty Creator, thank You for life and for the renewal and healing with which You bless me each day."

God created me and is constantly healing me.

Day 328

—◆—

*Courage is fear that
has said its prayers.*
—Dorothy Bernard

GROWING FAITH

When everything seems right in my world, I may feel that it is easy to have faith, and I do not question whether my life will continue to unfold in a positive direction. However, what happens when a crisis or a challenge comes along? Do I begin to doubt God's presence in my life?

I won't doubt when I remember that every challenge can be a new opportunity for growth and that even the smallest amount of faith on my part is enough to fuel tremendous courage—certainly enough to get me through whatever I need to get through.

My faith may seem small, but, like the tiny mustard seed, it contains astonishing potential for growth. And the more my faith grows, the more I rejoice over being in God's loving presence.

I have faith in God and in God's presence in my life.

Day 329

—◆—

Beloved,

You know the joy of letting My love live through you. Now you will never be satisfied in being anything less than an expression of love in the world. What a blessing you are!

You grow stronger and more confident each time we spend time together. Attentive to My voice, My guidance, you are alert to and follow through on the slightest stirring of a divine idea in your mind.

With every prayer, every life-affirming thought, you send a message of healing and renewal to the very cells of your body. You are ready and able to do truly magnificent things. Just as you have faith in Me, beloved, I have faith in you.

"We walk by faith, not by sight."
—2 Corinthians 5:7

Day 330

◆

Love is a fruit in season at all times,
and within reach of every hand.
—*Mother Teresa*

GOD
LOVES ME

God loves me! These three little words convey a powerful message that, when spoken aloud or held silently in my heart, infuse me with peace and joy.

Love is a gift from God, and the greatest gift I can give myself is to share the love of God within me with others. And I want to share the message of divine love with others.

Divine love is the answer to the questions of my heart. Whatever I seek—prosperity, health, order—I will find. I have all I need when I know that, out of love for me, God has already given all to me.

God's love for me will never lessen or fade away, for it is an eternal expression of caring by my Creator.

God loves me, and God's love for me
is eternal and without limitation.

Reaching Out to Children
By Marian Wright Edelman

I was jarred out of my thoughts by the ringing of the telephone! Discouraged that even in my role as a children's advocate I was not able to do more for children, I picked up the receiver. Then I heard, "Hi! This is Jeannie!"

Jeannie, in her forties now, was 13 when tragedy struck. During a drive-by shooting, someone fired a shotgun into the house where she lived. Jeannie was wounded in the eye. Because she had no health insurance, she was turned away by hospital after hospital. By the time her parents found one that would accept her, it was too late. She lost her eye.

I was outraged by the lack of access to health care for this child. Jeannie and I became good friends, and I was eventually able to help her get a prosthetic eye. She went on to finish school, have a family, and become employed by the Department of Human Services.

Talking to Jeannie that day, I was reminded of how much good can come from helping a child at the right time. The help I gave her was an investment in the future and in a wonderful mother and productive citizen.

Day 331

— ◆ —

As we use the light we have to the best
of our ability, more light comes.
—Marion R. Brown

LIGHT TOUCH A light, tender touch goes a long way toward comforting someone who is sad or upset. It soothes and supports; it shines the light of love and caring on them.

I can receive the "light" touch in any situation that threatens to overwhelm me or causes me to worry or become afraid. I do this by envisioning the light of God's presence continually surrounding me, bathing me in peace.

Enfolded in God's comforting presence, I realize that I am not alone. I and everyone I know—even those I don't know—are living in the presence of God.

With each breath, I breathe in the grace of God. In the light of God's love, I gain a true understanding of my spirituality and receive the assurance that all is well.

I am living in God's radiant light and love.

Day 332

◆

Every home takes on the quality of
the prevailing thought held in it.
—Myrtle Fillmore

HAVEN OF LOVE

Within every person there is a longing for home. And like everyone else, I want to live in a place where I am accepted, loved, and comforted. Such a longing is satisfied only when my home is built on the plan for a haven of love and peace that God has imprinted on my heart.

So whether I am living alone or with others, my heart's desire is to create a home where I gather with family and friends in an atmosphere of love and peace. And this is the atmosphere I help create with thoughtful, loving words and actions.

Such an atmosphere permeates the very walls of every room of my home, so that each person who enters feels embraced by acceptance, cheer, and goodwill.

My home is a haven of love and peace
for me and for all who enter there.

Day 333

—◆—

Joy is your gift from God, and it is not dependent on what occurred 10 years ago, a month ago, yesterday, or last night.
—Mary L. Kupferle

JOY OF SPIRIT

In as little as one day, I may experience many kinds of joy. The joy I feel when I see a loved one brings an immediate smile to my face. Or I may burst into laughter when I see or hear something funny.

And there is another kind of joy for me to experience as well—an inner joy that moves through my mind and body from the spirit of God within me. The intensity of such gladness is unmistakable, but also indescribable.

My whole body is engulfed by the joy of spirit, because I am aware of my own spirituality. Out of that joy, a new me is born.

The joy of spirit revives me and enlivens me. It is as if the spirit of God has touched every cell of my body and awakened each one to the joy of living. I am whole! I am a holy being filled with the joy of God!

The joy of spirit enlivens me now!

Day 334

◆

The soul is progressive. It must go forward.
The soul must meet and overcome its limitations.
—Stella Terrill Mann

SOUL JOURNEY

Since the moment I entered this physical realm, I have been searching to know more about why I am here. And one thing I know is this: My soul has answered the call to a journey that leads me to greater spiritual understanding.

Hope began this journey and faith sustains me along the way. In each step of the journey, I am accompanied by the love and understanding of God. I am gently, yet unfailingly, guided.

My journey is one of soul satisfaction, of moving forward in a greater awareness of who I am and what I am about. I am not driven by desperation, but rather I am inspired by a dedication to expressing God's life, love, and understanding.

**I am on a journey that brings me soul satisfaction
and spiritual understanding.**

Day 335

◆

The way I see it, if you want the rainbow,
you gotta put up with the rain.
—Dolly Parton

WONDER Oh, the wonder of a child! It is a combination of excitement and expectation, a certain knowing that the most wonderful event one could ever imagine is about to happen. Not even a shadow of a doubt gets in the way of a dream and its fulfillment.

The child is able to see the glory of God and, without the slightest hesitation, reaches out with open arms to accept it all. Somehow, without even being told, the child knows to look past circumstances and conditions to the unconditional love and acceptance of God.

And the truth about me is that I am a child, also—a child of God. I, too, open my arms and embrace each day in childlike wonder. I accept and give thanks for every blessing in the kingdom of God.

I embrace the blessings of God in childlike wonder.

Day 336

— ◆ —

Beloved,

As you join Me in the silence of prayer, open your heart and soul to all the beauty that you are, to the glorious wonder of all that you are experiencing right now. You are alive with My energizing life, and I am blessing you with a joy and peace that will soothe your soul and uplift you as you prepare for the hours, days, months, and years ahead.

We are ever one, beloved, and your presence in the world is vital to the well-being of so many. Never forget how valuable you are, how important your contribution is. The world would not be the same without you.

You are a sacred part of all that I have created. Live in the circle of My love. And then, through our divine connection, you will come to understand the truly priceless gift that you are— one of My gifts to the world.

"You are precious in my sight,
and honored, and I love you."
—Isaiah 43:4

Day 337

◆

The universe has an infinite capacity of givingness
for you, but you must develop your capacity
to receive and use its gifts.
—Rebecca Clark

GIFTS

As a child of God, I have been given gifts that have helped shape me and make me uniquely me. These gifts are mine to use, to enjoy, and to share with others.

A gentle smile, a cheerful hello, a helping hand, a loving hug—these are all gifts I can give to those in need of encouragement.

Perhaps my calm presence will make the difference when a young child needs reassurance or when a friend needs a boost in confidence to accomplish something. Just knowing I am there to love and support them may be the best gift I can give to them.

Whatever my own special gifts may be, I know that they have been given to me by my loving Creator to enjoy and to share.

> **I have special gifts to give, and I give them**
> **with a glad heart.**

Day 338

◆

For fast-acting relief,
try slowing down.
—Lily Tomlin

TIME OUT One of the most important times of the day is when I have a chance to relax. But even when I do not have the opportunity to actually stop everything I am doing, I can still take a time out—a relaxation break that stirs my awareness of the presence of God.

So I take a moment now to relax. If I am sitting, I allow the chair to support me; if I am standing, I focus on God's presence until I feel the tension leave my body. Now I take a deep breath and allow the breath of God to fill my lungs and spread throughout my body.

As I exhale slowly, I clear my mind and allow the spirit of God to take me into a moment of silence where, breathing gently, I can bask in the glory of God's presence. Then, slowly, I come back. I am relaxed, for I have taken time out to be totally in God's presence.

I take time out for a relaxation break
with God—every day.

Day 339

◆

*The whole being, when the law of forgiveness
is satisfied, draws new life and strength and power
from the one divine source and throws off the old.*
—*Cora Dedrick Fillmore*

**FOCUS
ON NOW**

How can I forgive a hurt so deep that even the passing of years has not dimmed its effect upon me? I begin by turning the entire situation over to God. God knows my pain, and God knows how to help me release the past so that the pain will also go away.

God is my strength, and with God I have the courage to release the past. I am now fully in this moment, this time of new opportunity and achievement. And I begin to understand that every experience has led me to where I am right now.

So I am able to forgive. And I feel such relief that I wonder why I carried any unforgiveness around with me. I feel lighthearted and ready to move on.

I release the past and forgive.

Day 340

———◆———

The more I traveled, the more I realized that fear makes strangers of people who should be friends.
—Shirley MacLaine

UNITY

I dedicate this day to putting aside any thought about how I may differ in opinion, belief, or appearance from the people in my family, my workplace, and my world.

Now I focus on what I have in common with all people—our spiritual connection. This is a bond that unites me with every person on Earth. God is the sacred spirit that lives in us and unites us all. When I know this truth and live it in my life, my relationships are ones in which there is mutual reverence, love, and caring.

Knowing that I am one in spirit with the people whom I live, work, and share the planet Earth with prepares me for meaningful, long-lasting relationships. With this understanding, I will always choose to be aware of my spiritual connection with others.

**God's spirit unites me with all people
in a sacred connection.**

Day 341

—◆—

The peace of every person on Earth is here now,
but it takes vision to bring it into visibility.
—Sue Sikking

WORLD PEACE   Peace is an ongoing process, and although it may not be achieved overnight, it can grow day by day, person by person.

World peace means more than just the end of all turmoil. It is love that nourishes and sustains. It is faith that continues to grow from person to person and remains strong from generation to generation.

I may have no road map to world peace, but I don't need one, for God will guide my actions and words. When I am at peace with myself, I will be peaceful toward all people.

Peace comes about as individual by individual believes that it is possible and perseveres until it is a reality for all. With the energy of a world of people directed toward peace, unrest withers and is blown away.

God is the source of world peace—of all peace.

Day 342

——◆——

Success is often achieved by those who
don't know that failure is inevitable.
—Coco Chanel

THE BEST ME The beginning of a new year is traditionally a time to set goals and make changes in life. However, I can set goals and make changes at any time. I may or may not stay with the goals I have set, but they give me something to work toward and provide a measure for my success.

Whatever my personal goals may be, the most important decision I can make is to be the best I can possibly be in this moment. I can only live in the now, not in the past or the future. Because I know this, I live fully and completely in the present.

There is no guarantee that I will reach every goal I set, but I receive great satisfaction from letting God's love be the motivation for all that I do. And with God's love moving me forward, there is always something of excellence to achieve!

I resolve to be the best me I can be!

Day 343

—◆—

Beloved,

You are My precious child. Let Me fill your mind with the unlimited possibilities that are available to you now. Listen, and I will reveal how you can use new ideas in exciting ways.

Follow the way I am showing you and discover the wonder of who you really are: My beloved creation. Nothing will be impossible for you when you learn that you can let go of what is no longer in your best interests. So let My light shine in and through you, for it will cast a glow of love all around you.

Every hour of every day, you are unfolding more and more of your true identity: a spirit-filled being of life and love.

"Strive for the greater gifts. And I will show you a still more excellent way."
—1 Corinthians 12:31

Day 344

◆

True wisdom does not consist only
of knowing, but of doing as well.
—*Martha Smock*

GOD
GUIDES
ME

I may receive all sorts of advice from well-meaning friends and family, from thoughtful-sounding experts and books. So my dilemma is often in trying to make the one right choice from so much information. How do I decide what is best for me?

I turn to the depths of my soul. In the quiet of my being, I know that God is my answer. Here, in the presence of the Creator, I receive ideas that resonate as a "yes" within me. The answers I was so busily seeking outside were always here within me.

In this sacred meeting with God, I hold nothing back. I give every bit of doubt, every concern and fear to God to be transformed into new faith and courage.

My guidance from God is just what I need to know—when I need to know it.

In the quiet of prayer with God, I receive ideas
that enrich my life.

Day 345

♦

I keep my ideals because in spite of everything,
I still believe that people are really good at heart.
—Anne Frank

THROUGH EYES OF LOVE The more loving I am to others, the more of God's love I am letting move out into the world through me. My heart beats with the rhythm of divine love so that my actions are in accord with the loving actions of others. Together we are praying for and working toward bringing more love into the world.

My first step is to take a closer look at my own attitudes and beliefs. Through eyes of love, I see what adjustments need to be made and then follow through with the divine guidance I receive in making those changes.

Now I am ready to accept other people just as they are. There is so much beauty and diversity in all humankind, and with my acceptance, I am truly beholding everyone through the eyes of divine love.

The love of God within me brings harmony
to all my relationships.

Day 346

---◆---

Keep your gaze upon the light and you cannot possibly see any darkness. When you are looking toward the light, shadows fall behind you.
—Myrtle Fillmore

BEING OF LIGHT

God created me, and I am a being of light and energy. As I speak words of life and healing, the response of every fiber of my mind and body is a resounding "yes" to life.

I am love and peace. I feel a divine inner prompting to share love and the peace that comes from knowing God's greatness with all people.

I am pure energy and lightness of being, capable of tremendous accomplishments. I live up to my divine capabilities by having the confidence to meet each challenge with faith and then having the faith to greet each opportunity with eager anticipation.

I am a being of light and energy, one of God's beloved creations.

Day 347

—◆—

*Nonresistance is
the path to freedom.*
—Marion R. Brown

**SOFT
ANSWER**
My first reaction to what someone
has said or done may not be
appropriate or even true to how I feel
just a few moments later—when I
have had time to think things over. So I know not to let
my first reaction overpower me.

Through nonresistance and a soft answer, I decide
what I say and how I feel. What a glorious feeling I
experience in being true to myself!

My nonresistant attitude acts as a filter that keeps the
anger and judgment of others from adversely affecting
me. And because I am nonresistant, I value the rights of
others to voice their own thoughts and beliefs.

My soft answer is a statement to myself and others
that I am living with the peace of God within me. I
contribute to the harmony in my relationships when I
speak to others from that inner peace.

**I speak words of kindness that resonate
from my peace-filled soul.**

Day 348

◆

Through practice, we learn to feel the presence
of God working in and through us at all times,
no matter what we are doing.
—May Rowland

KNOWING GOD
The greatest joy in my life is knowing the presence of God. I cannot help but feel complete when I know my oneness with Spirit.

Spiritual joy is more than just a passing emotion: It is a part of me that enhances my total well-being. Being fully in the presence of God fills me with a joy of spirit that uplifts me and lingers with me to bless what I am doing.

Joy is a precious gift from God, a gift I naturally want to share with others. The friendly smile on my face holds within it a spark of joy that can transform another person's face into an image of warmth and friendliness.

Yes, I am filled with joy because I am filled with the spirit of God. And my joy increases as I share it with others.

I am filled with joy because I am filled
with the spirit of God.

Day 349

—◆—

I think these difficult times have helped me to understand better than before how infinitely rich and beautiful life is in every way, and that so many things that one goes around worrying about are of no importance whatsoever.
—Isak Dinesen

MY SOURCE Although I may or may not consider myself materially wealthy, I know that money and possessions do not guarantee happiness. So what is the secret of prosperity?

As in all other matters, I find the source of my prosperity within me. God has blessed me with a spirit so that I experience true prosperity. I do not limit myself by measuring my prosperity by how many financial assets I have or how much property I own. I am aware of God within me and God within the world. This awareness brings peace and joy to everything I experience.

Every ending holds the promise of a new beginning. And each new day is an opportunity to receive new blessings from God.

God blesses me with the abundance of spirit.

DAILY WORD FOR WOMEN

Day 350

—◆—

Beloved,

Consider Me as your loving parent, for I am. When you have questions in your heart and mind, turn to Me for the answers. And if the situation does not seem to work out the way you would have liked, know that it is not because I did not answer your prayers—it could be that your desires were not in your best interests.

Trust in My judgment, beloved. In all things, let My love embrace you. Live your life as a celebration of the blessings I give to you.

Always know that you are loved by Me and blessed by My presence. Feel My loving spirit surrounding you. My love for you will never be withheld and will forever be unconditional.

"It is that very Spirit bearing witness with our spirit that we are children of God."
—Romans 8:16

Day 351

—◆—

Today a new sun rises for me; everything lives,
everything is animated, everything seems to speak to me
of my passion, everything invites me to cherish it.
—Anne de Lenclos

I Am
Praying

Worrying about loved ones never helps them, and it leaves me feeling helpless. On the other hand, my prayers for loved ones generate a spiritual energy that is powerful in blessing them and comforting me. Prayer is the way to bless others and find comfort for myself.

"God, there is no distance, no challenge, no solution that is beyond Your presence and power. You move as a soothing, healing current of energy through the very cells that give substance and form to my loved ones. You are with them to heal them, guide them, inspire them, and calm them.

"Thank You, God, for the assurance of Your love and caring—for me and those for whom I pray."

Thank You, God. Your presence heals, guides,
and inspires my loved ones.

Day 352

—◆—

What is right for one soul may not be right
for another. It may mean having to stand on your own
and do something strange in the eyes of others.
—Eileen Caddy

SACRED GROUND Loving Spirit, show me the way. Show me the way so that I can be a true example of love, faith, and understanding.

Guide my steps in matters of home, employment, and relationships so that I am right for the circumstances and they are right for me.

I open my eyes, my ears, and my heart to Your guidance, which may be a whisper, a feeling, or the certain knowing of a divine idea.

I know that the very ground on which I stand at any time is sacred, for wherever I am, Your presence is with me. I am ready to share Your message of love.

Awaken me to the sacredness of my soul so that I know my right place is wherever I am—as long as I am aware of Your presence.

God is leading me to my right place.

Day 353

—◆—

Love yourself first and everything else falls
into line. You really have to love yourself
to get anything done in this world.
—Lucille Ball

SPIRITUAL DISCOVERY   Freedom is more than a condition that exists for me in some or most matters. Freedom is the very essence of my being and moves from within me out into my life.

I free my mind of past hurts or negative remembrances and allow my soul to reach new heights of spiritual discovery. I free my body by ending harmful habits.

God has not set any limitations on me. I have the freedom to try new things and to be all that I can be. And if I do happen to make mistakes, I consider them merely learning experiences that help me know how I can do better next time.

I enthusiastically proclaim, "I am free!"

Thank You, sweet Spirit, for my freedom.

Day 354

—◆—

*Remember that you, too, are a marvelous creation,
filled with light and life and love and power. You are
unique to the world, special in your own way,
and important to humankind.—Deborah L. Cameron*

TRANQUIL SOUL In the innermost part of my being, there is a sacred place where no outer turmoil can intrude, where no feelings of doubt or failure can reside. Here, within the sanctuary of my soul, is the peace of God.

The peace of God passes all understanding. It is a feeling of well-being that gently erases any concern and brings comfort to my soul. Like the cool, tranquil waters of a mountain stream, divine peace refreshes me and eases even the deepest emotions.

There is peace within me that I can draw upon at all times, for God's spirit is always within me. In God's loving presence, I can have no doubt. And without a doubt, I have all the understanding and assurance that I need in order to live my life enfolded in the peace of God.

I live my life completely in the peace of God.

Day 355

◆

There are only two ways of spreading light—
to be the candle or the mirror that reflects it.
—Edith Wharton

RELIEF I feel such immediate relief when I finally set down a heavy load of groceries or a cumbersome object. I breathe easier, my muscles relax, and my steps become lighter when I free myself of the burden I was carrying.

And I feel relief when I forgive also, because I free my mind and heart of burdens I may have been carrying for days, weeks, months—even years. Through forgiveness, I let go of the past and make a conscious effort to step forward into a time of new opportunities and new growth.

And is it any wonder that my act of forgiveness causes me to walk lighter, to breathe easier, and to be more relaxed? By forgiving myself and others, I stand straighter and I move with confidence into a bright new future.

As I forgive, I release the burdens of the past.

Day 356

---◆---

Holding on to images of imperfection is like walking up a rough, steep hill. You don't get very far before you are worn out from your labor. Release the thoughts that spend your energies and make you struggle. Hold on to thoughts of life and perfection.—Peggy Pifer

INDIVIDUALITY

It is a well-known expression that no two snowflakes are alike. However, when I consider all creation, I realize that no two things are exactly alike. Each person, place, or thing created by God has been blessed with individuality.

Twins, triplets, even quadruplets may look alike, but each has his or her own thoughts, experiences, and perceptions. All people are unique creations of God with distinct personalities.

When I look at my loved ones and myself, I am able to perceive what is beyond physical appearance to the divinity that is within.

**God has blessed me with the gifts
of spirituality and individuality.**

Day 357

Beloved,

There is an energy filling the air, and it is the movement of My spirit through all people and all creatures. My energy is all-powerful, yet it is gentle—as gentle as the lightest touch of a breeze caressing a delicate flower. And this same energy moves through you and surrounds you in every moment.

The ground that you walk on has been touched by generations of people before you, and all have been in My care and keeping. I transcend all time, for I am eternal.

Tap into My energy and discover new levels of spiritual awareness. You are living in the now—a time of endless possibilities and new awakenings.

You can do and be all that you desire, for My energy is moving through you now as strength, peace of mind, and self-confidence.

"Not by might, nor by power, but by my spirit, says the Lord of hosts."
—Zechariah 4:6

Day 358

———◆———

Reach high, for stars lie hidden in your soul.
Dream deep, for every dream precedes the goal.
—Pamela Vaull Starr

SURRENDER TO GOD

How often do I hold back when attempting to accomplish a goal or a dream because I question whether I am smart enough, brave enough, or prepared enough?

I may have convinced myself that I am taking on the world single-handedly when the truth is that the real power and wisdom to do whatever I am to do is not determined by me; it is accomplished through the spirit of God within me.

So as I surrender my whole self to the activity of Spirit, the only thing I am giving up is fear. What tremendous relief I experience when anxiety or fear of failure is replaced by my faith in God working wonders through me. And I know that the greatest success I can have is in letting the spirit of God express through me in everyday and monumental matters.

I surrender myself to the creative power of God.

Day 359

———— ◆ ————

A woman is like a tea bag: You never know
her strength until you drop her in hot water.
—Nancy Reagan

ENERGY OF SPIRIT   There is an eternal spirit of life within me that springs from the very Spirit which created me. Like a stream of healing water, Spirit flows into every area, every cell of my mind and body. Rejuvenating life is an integral part of me.

I am refreshed! Each time I enter into an awareness of the spirit of life within, I am cooperating with healing energy. In tune with Spirit, I glow with life—life that renews every cell, every organ, every system of my body.

God's spirit within is my source of life! And with all my mind and heart, I believe in the divine plan for my body's capacity to heal. I am imbued with the spirit of life—the ever-renewing life of God.

God's spirit within is my source
of life and renewal.

Day 360

—◆—

Opportunities are usually disguised
by hard work, so most people don't recognize them.
—Ann Landers

COMMITMENT Each day brings new opportunities, and with those opportunities come new commitments—to myself and to the ones I love. However, the most important commitment I can ever make is to God— a commitment to live the truth I know and to stand firm in my belief that God is always with me.

How do I live my commitment to God? I live it through my actions—toward myself and others. I live it through love—by being the most loving person I can be and by treating myself and others with respect.

God's children deserve the very best. And whether giving my best means being more understanding or more accepting or simply more available to listen, I am willing. Being God's loving child is a commitment to God and to all God has created.

I am God's loving child, committed
to God and to all God has created.

Day 361

◆

Life isn't a matter of milestones,
but of moments.
—Rose Kennedy

I REST

I have no doubt about some things in life being complete and finished. I feel confident about moving on to a new home or job, moving forward in a plan or a relationship.

Yet at other times I may just need to give it a rest, to stop trying to force something to happen and trust that God is moving in a mighty way to bring about a blessing. This rest allows the situations and relationships to be resolved and refreshed.

And in this time of rest, I listen for divine guidance—the gentle thought that nudges me on in giving more time and energy to something or in calling it "complete." Going through any time of change, I will discover new strength because I am relying on God for the answers to all the questions that come up along my way.

I rest, knowing that God is moving
in a mighty way to bless me.

Day 362

—◆—

*Never doubt that a small group of thoughtful
citizens can change the world. Indeed, it
is the only thing that ever has.*
—Margaret Mead

**BREAKING
BARRIERS**
If I am having a problem getting
along with someone, I may be so
focused on what is wrong with the
relationship that I overlook what is
right with it. Yet some simple difference between
myself and the other person may begin to grow and
eventually push us apart.

Remembering that the presence of God is within all
people breaks the barriers of differences and allows a
circle of love and acceptance to draw me closer to
others. My relationships are founded on the belief that
there is one family of God, and because of this, my
relationships will flourish.

My inner spiritual nature will bring harmony,
understanding, and acceptance to my relationships.
Opinions and differences make all people unique, but it
is the oneness of spirit that unites me with all people.

**God is the spirit of love, understanding,
and acceptance that unites us all.**

Day 363

———◆———

Love is the emblem of eternity;
it confounds all notion of time.
—Anna Louise de Staël

ATMOSPHERE OF LOVE In the comfort of Your presence, God, I am enfolded in love. Your love conveys total and unconditional acceptance of me. Knowing that I need never do anything to earn Your love is a tremendous catalyst for letting all the love I possibly can live out through me. Because I do, I express the sacredness of Your love.

What a relief I feel in Your presence, God. Love rushes in and through me to heal every wound of body and emotion. When everything and everyone seems to be pressing in on me, Your love acts as a buffer that keeps me from being overwhelmed. I can breathe deeply and think clearly as I make decisions in peaceful moments or in a crisis.

God, You are my constant source of life and love, so I can and do move forward. Knowing that I am living in an atmosphere of Your love, I am comforted.

I am living in an atmosphere of God's love.

Day 364

—◆—

Beloved,

Not all gifts are simple ones to accept and take responsibility for. The gift of life is one that you have accepted, one in which you will experience emotional ups and downs.

But your faith will serve as a lifeline from you to Me. When you are in need of support, you will find the peace of mind you seek by remembering that you are always in My presence.

You may not be able to see Me, but I am there. I am in the wind that blows across the earth. I am the smile on the face of a loved one. I am in the hug of a happy child. I am love that transcends all boundaries and is available to all people.

Yes, your life is a gift that will bless many people. You are an example to people who are still seeking the kind of peace that fills your heart. I have given you the gift of life—not only to bless you, but also to bless the world.

"Out of the believer's heart shall flow rivers of living water."
—John 7:38

Day 365

◆

Far away there in the sunshine are my highest aspirations.
I may not reach them, but I can look up and see their
beauty, believe in them, and try to follow them.
—*Louisa May Alcott*

READY, WILLING, AND ABLE! This seems an especially appropriate time to prepare myself for the wonder and opportunity ahead. And one of the best ways I can prepare is through prayer:

"God, I am ready to carry out Your divine plan for me. Excitement about the adventures that await me builds so that I am filled with great expectation.

"God, I am willing to follow Your guidance. I look forward to what I will be experiencing with eager anticipation. I listen for Your guidance so that I am where I need to be, doing what I need to do. I am able to accept each blessing because I am prepared to be blessed. I am spiritually awake—open to all that You have to offer me. I joyously embrace life and all its wonders."

I am ready, willing, and able
to be blessed by God.

THE POWER OF LOVE

BY CHERYL LANDON

E arly childhood was a time of great challenge for me. My parents were divorced, and Mom worked full time to support us both. I felt so alone and somehow came to believe that there was something wrong with me because I did not fit into my world.

Then, when I was seven years old, Michael Landon married my mother and filled my world with unconditional love. He was my knight in shining armor and taught me to believe in myself and in the power of love. Dad sensed in me what he had faced most of his life—emotional darkness. At the time, I did not know that my new father had had an incredibly sad childhood, but we bonded immediately.

I learned to spread my wings and to trust. Dad filled the role of a spiritual teacher and was the best father I could ever have prayed would come into my life. He was a gift.

Like my mother, Dad was always there for me, and at age 19 I needed them more than I had ever before needed them. I was in a terrible car accident that left me in a coma. When my parents arrived at the hospital, I was in the ICU—so badly injured that they did not recognize me. They were told by the doctors that I probably would not live.

Mom and Dad did the only thing they knew to do: They prayed. During that prayer time, my father made a promise to God. When he and Mother returned to ICU, he began coaching me, telling me not to give up: "Fight, baby, fight!" Despite my lack of response, Dad continued to coach me. Mom and Dad held a vigil by my side until I awoke on the third day. I told Dad I had heard him calling me back while I was in the coma.

Dad's promise to God was a turning point for him. These are his own words: "I promised God that if he would let her live, I would do something useful with my life, something to make the world a little better because I'd been there. Cheryl lived, and I've tried to keep that promise ever since."

And Dad kept his promise to God by writing a universal message of spirituality into all his television stories. His promise touched millions of lives. In every series he produced, including *Little House on the Prairie* and *Highway to Heaven*, he expressed the things he most deeply believed. He believed in God, in family, in truth between people, and in the power of love. He believed that we really are created in God's image, and that God's spirit is within us all.

Twenty-one years after Dad made his promise, I was at his bedside. The doctors had told him he had only

DAILY WORD FOR WOMEN

three weeks to live. He said, "You know, Cheryl, I cannot die. Society is destroying itself, and I can make a difference." He had started a series called *Us* that was to address relationships and the power of love. Dad believed, as I do, that he had the potential to touch millions of people through this series.

Dad was too weak to get out of bed, so I lay down next to him, held his hand, and made a promise to him. He squeezed my hand when I told him I was going to carry on his message of love.

I had not yet read about his promise to God, but I would—in *Life* magazine—later that day. I think both our promises are about the power of love. I am a teacher and a writer, but I so believe that love can make our world a better place that I have become a speaker.

The greatest legacy parents can leave to their children is one of love, and that is the legacy my father and my mother gave to me. It caused me to reach out in love to people across the country and across the world.

Like Dad, I want people to believe in God and to have hope. We are all gifts of God. We are all miracles. Sometimes we just forget, and I am here to remind us that we are all message bearers. We all have the power of love within us, for we are all created in the love of God.

ABOUT THE
FEATURED AUTHORS

God's Gift of Life! (pg. 220)—Maya Brandenberger is an ordained Unity minister who is currently serving at Unity by the Sea in Santa Monica, California. Maya and her family reside in a rural canyon just outside of Los Angeles.

The Gift of God's Love (pg. 251)—Lynne Brown, director of Silent Unity, the prayer ministry of Unity School of Christianity, is an ordained Unity minister. She has served Unity School in various capacities for 20 years. Lynne, her husband, Kirk, and their children, Jessica and Zachary, enjoy country living in their Missouri farm community.

A Second Chance (pg. 156)—Sister Mary Rose Christy has worked as a religion teacher, nurse, advocate, social case worker, and lobbyist. She has been active in designing programs for work in areas of health, welfare, legal services, and youth—for which she has received numerous awards. She was the first official intern in the Arizona state legislature in 1970.

The Healing Gift of Laughter (pg. 93)—Phyllis Diller is a world-renowned comic of television, movies, and stage. She has authored four best-selling books and appeared as a piano soloist with over 100 orchestras. Phyllis has received Ph.D. degrees from Christian University in Dallas, and from Bluffan College and Kent State University, both in Ohio.

Reaching Out to Children (pg. 346)—Marian Wright Edelman, founder and president of the Children's Defense Fund, is a graduate of Spelman College and Yale Law School. She has served as director of the Center for Law and Education at Harvard University. A successful author, Marian has received many honorary degrees and awards, including the Albert Schweitzer Humanitarian Prize.

The Power of Words (pg. 125)—Mary-Alice Jafolla, former director of Silent Unity, is an ordained Unity minister. She is the author of *The Simple Truth*, and co-author with her husband, Richard, of *Nourishing the Life Force, The Quest, Adventures on the Quest, Quest '96, Quest '97,* and *Quest 2000*. Mary-Alice is also the co-author of numerous pamphlets, national magazine articles, and several cassette tapes.

The Power of Love (pg. 382)—Cheryl Landon is the eldest daughter of the late actor Michael Landon. The mother of one son, James Michael, she is an educator, lecturer, and author of the book *I Promised My Dad*. Cheryl is establishing the Landon Center for Higher Learning and Possibility Thinking.

A Glimpse of the Eternal (pg. 315)—Joan Lauren is a nationally acclaimed photographer who is noted for her beautiful natural-light portraits. Joan's photography has appeared in *Bazaar, Redbook,* and *Interview*. Her book, *Portraits of Life, with Love,* is a photo essay of celebrities who share their personal reflections on life and love.

The Brighter Outcome (pg. 187)—Jayne Meadows, who was born in China to missionary parents, is an accomplished actress of stage, screen, and television. Jayne is an active member of an entertainment industry that includes her husband, actor Steve Allen, and son, producer Bill Allen.

Love Heals (pg. 62)—Jessie O'Neill is founder and director of the Affluenza Project. She is a licensed therapist in Wisconsin, holds a masters degree in psychology and counseling, and is a member of the American Society of Experiential Therapists. As the author of *The Golden Ghetto: The Psychology of Affluence,* she makes frequent national radio and television appearances.

Creating a New Life of Love (pg. 282)—Dee Wallace Stone graduated from the University of Kansas in Lawrence, majoring in English and Education. She taught high school until her acting career was launched. Since that time, she has played in numerous television and film roles, including the 1982 blockbuster film *ET: The Extra Terrestrial.* Between roles, Dee teaches an acting class and does various charity work on behalf of children, animals, and women.

Giving Unconditional, Uncritical Love (pg. 31)—Betty White's husband, Allen Ludden, would teasingly introduce her as "My wife, a pioneer in 'silent' television." Betty is, indeed, a pioneer in television, starring in such hit television series as *Life with Elizabeth, The Mary Tyler Moore Show, The Golden Girls,* and *Maybe This Time.* Betty has received five Emmys and was inducted into the Television Academy Hall of Fame in 1995.

ABOUT THE FEATURED AUTHORS

INDEX

Acceptance, 34, 163, 166, 197,
    361, 368, 372, 378
Addiction, 17, 34, 47, 48, 56, 70,
    91, 107, 146, 200, 239, 249,
    289, 313, 333, 369
Aliveness, 87, 99, 104, 159, 160,
    190, 192, 196, 208, 327
Anger, 27, 53, 178, 191, 203,
    226, 242, 257, 303, 330, 338,
    348, 363
Awakening, 26, 50, 206
Awareness of God, 70, 73, 122,
    128, 131, 147, 153, 157, 202,
    252, 267, 300, 311, 350

Beauty, 36, 84, 119, 128, 170, 232,
    234, 268, 276, 287, 317, 337
Beginning, 10, 29, 37, 48, 50,
    120, 137, 186, 253, 262,
    282–84, 285, 300, 306, 313,
    314, 325, 376
Belief, 85, 115, 172, 333
Be still and know, 111, 116, 179
Blessing, 81, 86, 105, 109, 121,
    126, 143, 168, 170, 173, 185,
    219, 224, 226, 227, 241, 266,
    267, 281, 296, 303, 304, 322,
    328, 351, 356, 367, 369, 371
Breaking free, 70, 378
Breathing, 208, 347, 354

Caregivers, 168, 264, 329
Celebration, 130, 215, 255, 273
Challenge and crisis, 8, 33, 37,
    49, 88, 90, 96, 103, 107, 113,
    117, 172, 180, 194, 195, 197,
    204, 207, 214, 218, 229, 233,
    246, 249, 256, 259, 261, 263,
    274, 286, 295, 305, 307, 319,
    321, 343, 358, 369, 381
Change, 1, 5, 8, 33, 35, 47, 88,
    91, 98, 132, 136, 142, 164,
    186, 191, 218, 233, 239, 246,
    252, 261, 274, 280, 286, 313,
    319, 361, 378
Changing habits, 16, 17, 29, 34,
    47, 48, 56, 70, 91, 107, 146,
    200, 239, 249, 289, 313, 333,
    361, 369
Channels of blessings, 105
Children, 81, 156, 251, 336, 346,
    351
Clarity, 258, 265, 280, 288
Comfort, 11, 13, 51, 69, 113,
    122, 152, 195, 269, 276, 299,
    310, 345, 347, 379
Commitment to God, 151, 167,
    301, 376
Communion, 4, 39, 51, 72, 73,
    75, 106, 116, 135, 145, 161,
    211, 289, 297, 301, 335
Compassion, 95, 109, 169, 226
Confidence, 35, 111, 132, 208,
    237, 262, 280, 295, 302, 305,
    307, 325, 353, 362, 377
Confusion, 8, 20, 35, 88, 96, 111,
    114, 115, 202, 230, 244, 258,
    265, 280, 286, 298, 318, 319
Courage, 12, 16, 21, 26, 47, 108,
    124, 152, 222, 343, 360
Creativity, 9, 114, 117, 341, 374

Death, 282–84, 299, 306, 330,
    345, 347

Decisions, 38, 67, 103, 132, 193, 280, 287, 338, 360

Depression, 104, 117, 182, 190, 240, 255, 273, 320, 349

Despair, 21, 71, 152, 182, 184, 192, 194, 201, 216, 217, 221, 240, 249, 255, 265, 273, 293, 310, 320, 324, 332, 334, 349, 362

Diversity, 268, 292, 307, 326

Divine order, 19, 88, 96, 100, 102, 112, 136, 143, 158, 162, 204, 233, 234, 256, 261, 265, 271, 275, 280, 295, 298, 300, 308, 319

Divorce, 209, 299, 310

Doubt, 12, 38, 56, 68, 71, 72, 83, 112, 118, 120, 132, 148, 162, 170, 175, 183, 185, 192, 201, 207, 209, 217, 221, 230, 250, 258, 259, 280, 286, 290, 293, 301, 302, 324, 343, 351, 353, 360, 362, 370, 377

Dreams, 176, 213, 217, 278, 285, 325, 374

Emotional release, 235, 239, 247, 257, 279, 281, 304, 334, 348, 355, 370, 371

Energy, 89, 104, 159, 213, 217, 260, 373, 375

Enthusiasm, 117, 190, 209, 240, 327, 332

Expectations, 82, 137

Expression of Spirit, 69, 99, 289

Failure, 9, 120, 124, 127, 172, 197, 200, 214, 218, 221, 262, 277, 293, 306, 309, 355, 358

Faith, 10, 12, 16, 20, 26, 28, 33, 42, 45, 57, 59, 64, 68, 71, 72, 79, 83, 112, 115, 117, 118, 123, 145, 148, 162, 170, 175, 182, 193, 200, 217, 220, 229, 246, 256, 259, 271, 276, 286, 287, 301, 302, 305, 312, 316, 320, 323, 334, 343, 350, 357, 380

Family and friends, 40, 76, 85, 90, 105, 130, 151, 155, 166, 173, 184, 194, 202, 226, 235, 242, 245, 257, 281, 330, 336, 338, 341, 348, 356, 361, 367, 377, 378

Fear, 12, 35, 64, 66, 112, 118, 183, 185, 186, 198, 199, 214, 221, 229, 237, 242, 246, 250, 293, 334, 340, 343, 356, 360, 374

Forgiveness, 24, 60, 66, 72, 74, 77, 121, 150, 163, 173, 203, 226, 227, 257, 281, 304, 324, 330, 355, 369, 371

Foundation, 59, 270, 286

Freedom, 17, 19, 56, 70, 91, 127, 141, 154, 204, 222, 239, 290, 313, 333, 369

Gentleness, 169, 302

Giving, 353

Goals/Goal setting, 132, 207, 210, 217, 244, 259, 278, 280, 285, 290, 358, 374, 381

God's creation, 23, 127, 131, 317, 362, 372

God's gifts, 20, 21, 41, 74, 220, 380

Golden Rule, 53, 155, 242

Grace, 6, 20, 107, 108, 149, 156, 206, 224, 253, 276, 324, 340

Graduation, 132

Gratitude, 30, 74, 87, 94, 119, 141, 148, 161, 170, 182, 184, 224, 267, 276, 296, 320, 322, 328, 331, 336

Growing and unfolding, 21, 50, 98, 124, 131, 134, 142, 181, 215, 268, 302, 313, 359

Guidance, 5, 13, 35, 38, 52, 58, 61, 67, 68, 100, 103, 107, 111, 112, 120, 136, 138, 176, 183, 193, 209, 212, 214, 219, 228, 230, 253, 256, 258, 262, 265, 274, 287, 294, 302, 305, 312, 320, 344, 357, 359, 361, 366, 368, 377, 381

Harmony, 27, 53, 59, 78, 115, 133, 163, 178, 191, 205, 242, 275, 286, 292, 307, 338, 341, 348, 356, 361, 363, 378

Healing, 2, 19, 25, 55, 62, 63, 74, 89, 93–94, 99, 104, 108, 110, 130, 146, 147, 177, 181, 187–89, 196, 208, 234, 236, 260, 264, 271, 281, 304, 310, 314, 315, 327, 342, 344, 375, 379

Health and wholeness, 2, 25, 87, 147, 158, 177, 209, 279, 327, 332, 349, 371

Heart, 303, 342

Home, 348, 368

Hope, 3, 322, 328, 349, 350, 351, 352, 362, 370, 379

Humility, 321

Imagination, 133, 278, 303, 341

Individuality, 23, 41, 372

Inner beauty, 36, 84, 134, 232, 234, 268, 337

Inspiration, 67, 86, 159, 210

Joy, 22, 36, 46, 60, 80, 86, 161, 171, 184, 216, 255, 273, 291, 310, 315, 316, 332, 349, 364

Kindness, 44, 80, 92, 178, 233

Knowing God, 364

Laughter, 93–94, 255, 291, 310, 332

Learning, 197, 238, 241, 300

Let go, let God, 5, 33, 250, 298, 318, 334

Light of God, 114, 161, 175, 230, 262, 267, 347, 362, 371

Listening, 11, 36, 58, 65, 106, 111, 118, 180, 201, 211, 237, 243, 287

Living now, 47, 311, 331, 355, 367

Loneliness, 116

Loss, 209, 257, 282–84, 306, 310, 330, 345, 347, 349

Love, 3, 7, 11, 14, 31, 32, 36, 43, 45, 60, 62, 66, 76, 80, 81, 95, 102, 113, 137, 140, 149, 150, 160, 203, 215, 251, 264, 269, 296, 298, 299, 303, 342, 345, 351, 357, 361, 379

Loving and blessing others, 15, 23, 24, 40, 44, 53, 74, 76, 77, 78, 80, 81, 84, 86, 90, 92, 109, 143, 150, 155, 163, 168, 173, 185, 245, 266, 277, 292, 304, 307, 312, 326, 328, 329, 330, 333, 346, 356, 363, 367, 380

Memories, 37, 121, 235, 253, 304, 311, 331, 349, 355, 369, 371

Miracles, 52, 215, 220, 263, 293, 298

Moving, 70
Moving mountains, 68, 72

Nature, 119, 128, 136, 243, 317
Never alone, 102, 165, 174, 198,
   209, 212, 221, 263, 270, 277,
   299, 310, 323, 345

One in spirit, 23, 135, 275
One step at a time, 12, 229, 325
One with God, 4, 39, 51, 72, 73,
   75, 116, 135, 171
Opportunities, 376

Parents, 81, 151, 232, 336
Part of the whole, 88, 96
Past mistakes, 72, 121, 150, 253,
   281, 304, 355, 369, 371
Peace, 11, 25, 53, 54, 78, 89, 92,
   103, 113, 115, 129, 133, 145,
   165, 166, 178, 180, 195, 199,
   223, 237, 272, 288, 339, 357,
   370
Personal growth, 16, 98, 124,
   131, 134, 181, 252
Pets, 31, 126, 168, 194
Power and potential, 65, 68, 98,
   117, 124, 134, 139, 142, 176,
   190, 198, 212, 213, 229, 231,
   232, 233, 238, 254, 275, 290,
   294, 318, 373
Power of God, 39, 43, 65, 309
Prayer, 4, 5, 13, 15, 39, 58, 60,
   61, 63, 74, 75, 78, 79, 81, 82,
   83, 90, 94, 97, 106, 122, 137,
   138, 144, 153, 157, 162, 173,
   187–89, 243, 245, 247, 249,
   252, 269, 288, 305, 335, 336,
   352, 360, 367, 381
Preparation, 210, 285, 305, 381
Presence of God, 4, 22, 27, 32,

69, 73, 75, 82, 89, 111, 122,
   148, 153, 158, 164, 175, 211,
   221, 223, 231, 269, 272, 293,
   297, 299, 323, 340, 347, 354,
   364, 368, 378, 379
Prosperity, 30, 71, 133, 259,
   296, 316, 365

Quietness, 51, 83, 116, 157,
   179, 211, 269, 335, 339, 360

Recovery, 146
Refreshed, 75, 97, 159, 335, 337,
   375
Relationships, 20, 40, 60, 66, 85,
   107, 151, 155, 161, 166, 184,
   226, 228, 235, 242, 245, 257,
   262, 270, 281, 282–84, 299,
   356, 361, 377, 378
Relationship with God, 9, 14,
   106, 120, 122, 123, 144, 159,
   174, 219, 225, 270, 321
Relaxation, 22, 25, 26, 44, 63,
   75, 97, 129, 154, 196, 199,
   208, 210, 238, 272, 291, 295,
   332, 335, 354
Remembering God, 28, 29, 37,
   311
Rest, 18, 22, 59, 87, 97, 110,
   164, 167, 199, 205, 260, 271,
   285, 295, 314, 337, 375, 377
Reverence, 317

Sacredness, 13, 145, 297
Searching, 38
Security, 33, 165, 195, 227
Self-esteem, 34, 41, 57, 105,
   121, 124, 176, 192, 206, 207,
   231, 232, 239, 254, 292, 316,
   318, 324, 333, 344, 350, 352,
   353, 358, 369, 372

Self-forgetting, 46, 106, 203,
206, 225, 311, 355
Self-transcendence, 26, 49, 56, 91,
101, 207, 216, 225, 278, 279
Serving others, 41, 44, 155, 185,
312, 329, 333, 346, 353
Silence, 6, 157, 199, 230, 247,
252, 287, 297, 339, 352
Simplicity, 288
Sleep, 46, 97
Smile, 194, 255, 364
Speech, 27, 29, 32, 46, 55, 58,
60, 67, 77, 79, 85, 101, 104,
109, 110, 125, 129, 143, 147,
159, 177, 190, 216, 222, 235,
236, 254, 279, 290, 320, 334,
348, 349, 363
Spiritual journey, 26, 197, 325,
350, 369
Spiritual vision, 96, 228, 307
Strength, 14, 20, 25, 47, 51, 79,
99, 108, 139, 152, 160, 169,
180, 181, 213, 215, 246, 248,
312, 318, 321, 375
Stress, 103, 146, 210, 280, 288,
291, 295, 307, 318, 331, 332,
339, 347
Success, 75, 172, 202, 218, 309,
358, 365
Surrender, 16, 24, 45, 61, 64,
114, 141, 167, 200, 204, 225,
235, 241, 244, 274, 295, 298,
302, 334, 360, 374, 377
Sustaining power of God, 65,
102, 118, 172, 174, 180, 181,
248, 263, 277, 294, 308, 309,
321, 337

Thoughts, 27, 29, 32, 46, 55, 58,
60, 67, 77, 79, 85, 101, 104,
109, 110, 121, 125, 129, 143,
147, 159, 177, 190, 216, 218,
222, 235, 236, 248, 254, 279,
290, 320, 334, 348, 349
Time, 331, 337
Transformation, 1, 85, 324
True self, 90, 110, 176, 191, 198,
231, 232, 234, 243, 268, 289,
297, 315, 316, 321, 344, 352,
353, 358, 370, 372
Trust, 3, 7, 28, 45, 57, 64, 68,
72, 101, 123, 136, 141, 193,
205, 366
Turning point, 1, 10, 107, 164

Unconditional love, 3, 7, 11, 14,
24, 31, 32, 36, 60, 62, 66, 76,
95, 102, 113, 116, 123, 137,
138, 139, 140, 149, 150, 152,
160, 167, 174, 191, 201, 203,
205, 215, 219, 227, 240, 241,
247, 251, 270, 293, 296, 298,
299, 301, 303, 308, 316, 324,
326, 342, 345, 351, 352, 357,
361, 366, 379
Unity, 356
Unlimited possibilities, 127,
249, 277, 341, 359, 373

Vacations, 154

Wisdom, 20, 43, 103, 254, 258,
265, 278, 294, 320, 360
Wonder, 192, 206, 351
Work, 85, 143, 178, 186, 214,
228, 238, 242, 278, 295, 305,
332, 338, 341, 356, 368, 374
World peace, 53, 78, 133, 166,
178, 357
World vision, 53
Worry, 248, 250, 273, 298, 308,
334, 342, 360, 365, 367

INDEX